Praise for *Finding Jill* . . .

MW01031789

"Natives help one another as they have sha. understand. If you have experienced a significant loss, Jill's story can help you on your journey of healing."

—Bernie Siegel, MD
Author of *A Book of Miracles* and *Faith, Hope and Healing*

"*Finding Jill* is a gut-wrenching, unforgettable story of overcoming the most adverse conditions life can hand a wife and mother. If you're wondering where and how to begin to rebuild your life after a loved one's death, this book is a must read. If you have a friend who has experienced a loss, this book will help you identify. If you've ever wondered what loss feels like and what the capacity for healing is, you need to read this book."

—Rebecca Hauder, RN, MEd, LCPC, LMFT
**Author of *The Nature of Grief*
Owner of Resources for Grief**

"This book should be must-reading for everyone who experiences the sudden loss of a loved one or loved ones. It is a book of deep pathos and monumental courage. Jill could not have shown us how to grieve and survive our losses any better. The word that emerges through it all is *hope*."

—Bob Deits
**Author of *Life after Loss* and coauthor of *When Your Grandma Forgets*
(*Helping Children Cope with Alzheimer's and Beyond*)**

"*Finding Jill* is a must-read book for anyone who has ever lost a loved one, as well as those who seek to offer support. Jill Kraft Thompson's inspirational story is both heart-wrenching and heart-affirming, taking the reader on a journey from tragic loss to finding the hope and courage to live and love once again. In opening her heart, Jill allows us to gain a deeper understanding of the grief process and how to transform grief into strength."

—Barb Adams
Host, *Amerika Now* talk radio show

Finding Jill

How I Rebuilt My Life after Losing the Five People I Loved Most

Jill Kraft Thompson

MIND, BODY, AND SOUL
PRODUCTIONS
McCall, Idaho

Published by:

MIND, BODY, AND SOUL PRODUCTIONS
227 Morgan Drive
McCall, ID 83638
www.findingjill.net

Editor: Ellen Kleiner
Book redesign and production: Angela Werneke, River Light Media

Printed in the United States of America

PUBLISHER'S CATALOGING-IN-PUBLICATION DATA

Thompson, Jill Kraft.

Finding Jill : how I rebuilt my life after losing the five people I loved most / Jill Kraft Thompson. — McCall, Idaho : Mind, Body, and Soul Productions, c2013.

p. ; cm.

ISBN: 978-0-9894252-2-3 (print); 978-0-9894252-1-6 (ebk.)

Summary: Jill Kraft Thompson had a life filled with love. Then, in the middle of a two-year adventure in Italy for her husband's work, a semi truck plowed into their minivan, killing the five people most dear to her: her husband, their two young sons, her mother, and her niece, while barely surviving herself. In the course of her recovery journey, she realizes that while she will never forget her loved ones who have passed on, she can renew her faith and find room in her heart to live, and to love, again.—Publisher.

1. Grief. 2. Bereavement—Psychological aspects. 3. Loss (Psychology). 4. Families—Death—Psychological apsects. 5. Mental healing. 6. Bereavement—Religious aspects. 7. Hope. 8. Death—Psychological aspects. I. Title.

BF575.G7 T46 2013   2013940089

155.9/37--dc23   1309

1   3   5   7   9   10   8   6   4   2

To ALL INDIVIDUALS who have suffered through grief.

Whether it comes in a great mass or a minute spore, grief must be honored with thought, perseverance, and understanding so that it can be transformed into our strength rather than our weakness.

To MY HUSBAND BART,

who believed in me and gave me confidence and undying love.

AND TO MY HUSBAND JOHN,

who has held me up when I have not had the strength to stand on my own, and who has brought love, joy, and laughter into my life.

Thank you, loves of my life!

Acknowledgments

I AM GRATEFUL TO SHARON KATZ, who taught me how to find the tools to face my grief, stepped me through each situation, gave me permission to grieve my way, and helped me take control of my life again. Thank you for your guidance and continued support.

I also want to express gratitude to Kevin Quirk for making my dream of sharing my story a reality, using his talent as a writer to capture my voice, thoughts, feelings, and vision and to bring clarity and direction to a story I pray will help others; to Lisa Kraft, Martha Tikker, and Wayne Allan, for participating in the creation of this book; and to my friends and family who have loved and supported me these past years during my journey through grief.

Thanks, too, to Kelly Heindel, who threw me a lifeline of love and non-judgment each moment I felt I had no ability to continue. You, I love!

Finally, a special thanks to John and Franklin for listening to my endless stories about Bart, Benjamin, and Samuel, and for making them part of our family. Having your permission to carry the love I have for them has given me the ability to love deeper than I ever thought was possible. You both are my inspiration for living each day with happiness, acceptance, and love.

Contents

Prelude
The Mirror

I LOOK IN THE MIRROR *and see the image of a woman who has scars. Those on her neck and forehead are camouflaged by the foundation she has so carefully applied, while the other physical marks on her leg, arm, and shoulder are hidden by strategic placement of clothing and jewelry.*

But what about the scars on the inside, in her soul—the scars no mirror can hide? She looks lonely, frightened, lost, imprisoned by pain that borders on desperation. As I continue to look, I see the image of a woman who is alone and disconnected, struggling with grief recovery, existing but not really alive. She is a woman who dares not plan, not beyond a year, a month, a day, a minute. Because she knows that plans are never to be trusted, that they are a setup for despair. With each breath, she remembers that every plan, every hope for the future, can be wiped out in a split second, causing seemingly interminable grief and sorrow.

The woman in the mirror knows all this, but she also knows that other woman who used to look in the mirror not so many years ago, a woman able to plan, to dream, to seek. This other woman could see herself as a developing ceramic artist, or a personal decorator, or an accomplished golfer—all while relishing life with family and friends. This other woman's laughter, lightness, and unending love encircled her every move, and joy filled her being. The mirrored woman longs for this other woman to reappear. Occasionally, amidst the sadness and suffering, she catches glimpses of her in the shadows and experiences brief moments of levity and joy as she continues struggling to break free from grief and suffering. Will she ultimately surrender and allow grief to submerge her, sucking her beneath its giant unending wave, or will she somehow, someday find her way to calmer waters of peace and happiness, altering that image in the mirror? ⤳

Introduction

As MARCH 25, 2012, a milestone anniversary in my life, fast approached, I was not planning a festive celebration with decadent cakes or glittering presents. I was not inviting dozens of family and friends to share the moment with me at my home. I had no plans for dancing music, boisterous laughter, or champagne toasts. It was not that kind of anniversary.

As the big day drew near, I'd begun feeling so ill and tired that I was not getting up until 10:00 am or even noon. I'd canceled most obligations, and I was drinking a glass of wine every night just to numb the feelings of sadness that were starting to overwhelm me. I was planning on going out of town, to San Diego, for the anniversary date itself, to do something completely different to seek a buffer against the waves of grief and desperation.

Ten years before, on March 25, 2002, my life as I had known it ended. On a busy interstate in Italy, a semi truck lost control, crossed a median, and smashed headfirst into my family's minivan. My husband, my two young sons, my mother, and my niece all died. My sister and I survived, something no one who saw the photo of the wreckage could imagine. In one moment, everything I had known and loved had been taken away, and I couldn't understand why on earth I hadn't gone with them.

Finding Jill is the story of how I endured the unbearable pain, loss, and grief and underwent a gradual recovery so I could begin to truly live life again with hope and joy. What I have learned in these past ten years has filled my heart and soul. I have survived not only physically but also mentally, emotionally, and spiritually. I thank God for the strength and courage to stand with me every day, many of which have not been at all pretty. I feel deep gratitude for so many people who have reached out to me with love, caring, and compassion, even when I sometimes seemed to push them away.

Through telling about my own journey of grief recovery, I hope to help others who have suffered difficult losses, either recently or some time ago. It doesn't matter how many months or years have gone by; losses don't go away, and it is necessary to deal with grief. It's not important how loss occurred in others' lives, or who or what was a part of it, only that the loss is deeply felt. None of us can know exactly what other grieving people are feeling, but we can tell our story in the hope that others may benefit from our experiences.

This book does not begin with images of shattered glass and twisted metal but rather where my *real* story starts, with love, union, the building of a family, and dreams of a wonderful future. It then goes on to depict our adventure of living in Italy, where we became as close as any family could be, right up until those final days in Venice. To get across the true nature of my loss, it is necessary to portray my family and the depth of my love for those who died. Only then can others begin to grasp just how unbearable it was for me to wake up from surviving that horrible accident to learn I'd never see them on earth again.

The latter part of the book is a candid revelation of the twists and turns of my grief recovery and healing process, including descriptions of the tools and advice I found helpful; the inner resources I needed to tap; and the ways others assisted me during this journey. My deepest wish is that others may find in my personal account something that touches them or provides them with ideas, insights, or images that may light their own path forward during grief recovery. Any difference I can make in the lives of others will make an even greater difference in my own.

Chapter 1
The Ring

MOM HAD ALWAYS BEEN MY ANCHOR. I could come to her with any need, any problem to sort out, and she'd be right there with the answer I was looking for or the words I yearned to hear. That was true when I was a little girl in the small town of Weiser, Idaho. It was true after she and Dad divorced when I was thirteen and she had to go to work to keep us afloat. And it was still true when I was twenty-one, living in Boise and feeling lost.

I remember one night at her condo when I was feeling especially down and Mom supported my self-esteem. "Mom, I've had enough of adventure," I announced. "I want to figure out some kind of purpose, a clear direction to follow. But sometimes it just feels like I fail at everything I try."

She was aware of the evidence. After dropping out of the University of Idaho before the end of my sophomore year with poor grades, I had been drifting from place to place and job to job. I had tried working at an assisted living facility for the mentally challenged because I had intended to be a psychology major in college, but that didn't stick. I remember a big, burly man with MS had asked me to sneak him some Saltines, and when he began choking on them I had to pick him up and throw him hard on the bed to dislodge the crackers. Another time I was helping a patient get to the toilet and before I could get my gloves on he pooped on my hand. After yet another male patient whom I was trying to move grabbed my breasts and then giggled at what he had done, I quit.

I had also worked for a while at a Boise bank; followed some girlfriends up to Sun Valley one summer, where I sold tickets for the Sports Center and got to meet Jamie Lee Curtis; and finally spent seven months juggling jobs at an events center and a preschool in Coeur d'Alene. When my money ran out, Mom had told me, "You need to move back to Boise."

After coming back to Boise, I lived with Mom for a while, just as I had when I first dropped out of college. Even after I moved into an apartment with my stepsister Stacey, I still spent many a night at Mom's. By that time, I was employed in the Fine Jewelry Department of JC Penney at Boise Towne Square, and after work I'd head over to her place, where we'd pop popcorn and snuggle up on the sofa to watch TV together. On the night I was feeling like a failure, we were tuned in to *Northern Exposure*, one of her favorite programs.

"You are not a failure, and I am very proud of you," Mom insisted. "So you didn't finish college. Look at your friends who did graduate. They're not smarter than you. You don't need a degree to prove how smart you are. Learning is a never-ending process. Even in college you were learning."

"Right," I chuckled. "I was learning how to socialize! I guess I really don't believe I failed at school, but I'd just like to be going somewhere. Looks like my idea of becoming a jewelry designer isn't going to happen. So now where do I go?"

Mom laid her hand on my wrist and said, encouragingly, "Well, I know you, and I know that you will excel at whatever you choose to do. You will search until you find the one thing you truly love, and when you do you will follow it with all your heart."

I grabbed a handful of popcorn and thought a moment. "If I'm honest with myself," I said between bites, "that one thing is to be a wife and mother. But that doesn't seem very realistic these days, does it?"

Mom just smiled and moved closer to me on the sofa. We watched TV in silence.

I enjoyed my job at JC Penney, where I would assist women and men shopping for major gifts. Once I earned a company prize for selling the most watches, and as a reward I got to select my favorite Bulova. I was good at my job because I had taken time to educate myself about the kind of jewelry we carried. "If you study something to the nth degree, you will excel at it," Mom would say. I could look at a piece of jewelry and detect any defect in it, and sometimes I could even handle a repair myself so we wouldn't have to send it out. I also enjoyed doing my own engraving.

As with any jewelry department, engagement and wedding rings were a popular attraction for our customers. I always had my eyes out for rings that appealed to me personally, and one day my gaze fixed on a .30-carat brilliant-cut ring with little dazzling diamonds. It came in a round shape, but I was envisioning something a little more…me.

One day I asked the distributor, "Do you have one in a marquise setting?"

When she later brought one like that into the store, I held it in my hand and beamed. "That's my ring!" I proclaimed. "If someone wants to buy this ring, they'd better be sure they want to marry me."

I wasn't shy about telling my coworkers and friends of my decision. "Nice ring, Jill. Now you just need a husband to go with it. Hope you find one before that ring is taken," said Barbara, a regular at all the singles events in Boise.

"Don't worry, I will," I countered. "And whoever it is he better understand that the prongs have to be fixed. This ring has to be just right for me."

From that day forward, this ring with three brilliant-cut diamonds on each side, and a fourth to be added when it was converted to a wedding band, was known as "Jill's ring." We would all kid around about the idea, but in my soul I knew it was true. Just as I knew the first time I laid eyes on Barton Joel Kraft that this man was to be my husband.

My relationship with Barton began when I left JC Penney and began working in the escrow business. One evening after work Mom invited me to a singles event sponsored by The Beautiful Savior Lutheran Church, where she was an active member. I was not looking forward to going. Even though my older brother Steve and his girlfriend Mary would be there, I wouldn't know anyone else. And I wasn't feeling very attractive that day, having worn a skirt borrowed from Mom and feeling pudgy due to weight I had gained in college and had not been able to lose.

"Maybe I'll stay home," I said to myself. Then I shook my head and added, "No, I need to do this to support Mom. I'll just show up a little late."

Arriving with low expectations, I opened the door to Mom's house and suddenly found myself looking into the eyes of the most handsome man I had ever seen. And it just so happened that the only seat available was right beside him. *Mom, I love you*, I thought to myself. I began bantering nervously with the man of my dreams. I let him talk enough for me to learn that his name was Bart; he worked for Micron, the growing microchip firm that was a Boise mainstay; and that he was pursuing a master's degree to enhance his prospects there. This handsome man and I, along with Steve and Mary, were by far the four youngest people there, and when Steve suggested we go off to see a movie, I jumped at the idea.

"Great idea, Steve!" I burst out. "Let's all four of us go." I looked at Bart eagerly.

"Well, that does sound like a good idea," he began, "but it's getting late. I'm afraid I need to head home and study."

The color drained from my face. *Go home and study?* To me, that was the biggest rejection anyone could give. As far as I was concerned, if he was at all interested in me school would come second, which is how it had always been for me in college.

As I watched Bart leave, I decided that I would have to be satisfied with admiring the man of my dreams from afar, at least for a while. But since he had said he attended Mom's church regularly and had even begun to get to know Mom as a friend I made a sincere vow: I would forgo sleeping in on Sunday mornings and show up every week for the service at The Beautiful Savior Lutheran Church. "I'll just tell Mom I'm attending to strengthen my faith," I said to myself. "I'm not going to let anyone know I have my eyes on some man who doesn't seem interested in me!"

This is how I became a fixture at The Beautiful Savior Lutheran Church, although I already had a strong faith. I attended regularly with Mom and her boyfriend Dick, who drove the seventy-five miles from Weiser, where they had met and he still lived. At church, I would gaze discreetly at Bart now and then, and I found out more information about him: he had recently moved to Boise from the Seattle area and was newly divorced but had no children. The fact that he was divorced didn't scare me. I had learned from my parents, whom I both adored, that some people just do not work well together.

More than a year after that first look at this man I was secretly in love with, Mom organized another singles event—this one a picnic in a park. Again, I felt I had to attend so I wouldn't let Mom down. But I also figured it might be another occasion to at least talk to Bart. When I first arrived, I didn't spot him and joined in a kickball game. But soon I looked up to see Bart...and some other woman clinging to him! Instantly, I felt my knees buckle, convinced that I was on the verge of fainting, vomiting, or both. *He's cheating on me!* I thought. *I realize he barely knows my name, but still.*

"Mom, I need to go home," I muttered, feeling a deep sense of regret since she had driven me over and would need to drive me back. "I just feel sick all of a sudden."

"Honey, what's wrong?" she asked. "Can you sit down for a few minutes and see if it will pass? You know I'm in charge of this event. I would hate to leave so soon."

"Mom, I'm so sorry, but I think I'm going to throw up," I added with a sense of urgency, eager to get away from the disappointing situation.

Mom helped calm me briefly, and then, as she always had, she responded to my needs. On the drive home, she didn't even ask me the kinds of questions that might have made it too hard to conceal the truth. If she suspected anything about my crush on Bart, she never told me.

I was so deflated that I avoided our church for a while, but I couldn't stay away for long. My first time back Bart was there. And when he happened to join Mom, Dick, and me after the sermon on our way out the door, all of a sudden Mom invited him to play a round of golf with us—and he accepted! My knees buckled again, but this time I stood my ground. "I'll go kick his butt in golf," I said to myself. "That will show him I'm no typical girl."

We headed for Warm Springs, where Mom and Dick informed us that they could only play nine holes but asked Bart and me if we would like to play nine more. I thought, *Sure, no problem. He's just a golfing partner for the day. Oh, is that a hickey on his neck? Gross!* But when we finished the eighteen holes and said good-bye, I renewed my vow to go to church every Sunday, figuring God missed me!

Then one day out of the blue Bart called me at work. "Your mom gave me your number," he said. "I hope it's okay to call you."

"No problem," I said, still in my defiant mode.

"Well, my friend Pete and I have four tickets to the Jazz-Sonics basketball game at the Pavilion tonight. A couple of girls we know from Oregon were going to come with us, but they had to cancel. Pete got a friend to come, but her girlfriend can't make it. I know this is last minute, but I was wondering if you might..."

If I had really been defiant, I would have been thinking, *Why, the nerve of this guy. Who does he think he is?* But that wasn't exactly what I was thinking. "I'd love to come!" I gushed, my heart pounding out of my chest, forgetting I already had a date that night.

"Okay, we'll pick you up at six then," he responded, sounding just a bit surprised.

My mind was racing. He most likely had been dating others in the eighteen months since I had first seen him and decided I was going to marry him. But I had been flirting with and dating other men, too. I immediately picked up the phone and called my intended date, saying, "I'm really sorry, Mike. I forgot that I had plans with a friend from church." Well, at least the last part was true.

At the basketball game, I had no idea what was happening on the court, but things were proceeding quite well in the stands. I had no more weak knees. I was so confident in being around Bart that in a few weeks I invited him to my sister Jody's Halloween party. Bart accepted, but as the date drew near I got nervous and wondered if there really was someone else in his life and whether I would have to tell him it was okay to bring a "friend." Feeling self-protective, I chose not to follow through on the invitation. Little did I know that he sat by the phone that night, costume ready. I still feel bad I disappointed him!

Some weeks after the Halloween party, on Sunday, December 8, 1991, Jody and I went shopping at Boise Towne Square. As I had done on every visit to the mall since I had left my job at JC Penney, I made it a point to circle around to the jewelry counter to see if my ring was still there. It was. Usually, while with someone who had not seen it I would put on the ring and say, laughing, "If some guy walks by, he will know this is the ring I want." Jody had already heard that one, so I just said it to myself.

After we got back to Mom's condo, I began talking with Jody about my dating life. "You know, I don't really like Mike or Dan more than friends," I told her as I picked up the phone to check for messages on Mom's answering machine, as she had asked us to do. "I've never told anyone this, but the guy I really like is Bart Kraft. You can't tell him, though, because he doesn't really like me."

And then I heard the message: "Hi, this is Bart Kraft. I'm calling for Jill. Jill, I'm finishing my finals this week, and I was hoping you would go out and celebrate with me. Can I take you to dinner this weekend? Either Friday or Saturday works for me. Call me and let me know. Thanks!"

"It's him! It's him!" I shouted to Jody as I hopped around the kitchen.

I called Bart right back and accepted for Friday night—Friday the 13th. On the day of his celebration dinner, I took my time getting ready. Even though I didn't drink wine at the time, I drank a glass of Mom's Riesling to calm my nerves. Bart picked me up in his gold Porsche, looking very hot! He took me to B. B. Strand's, a small restaurant in downtown Boise where the tables were covered with paper. When Bart colored some pictures for me, I thought, *How romantic!* And when he chose an entrée with shark even though I detest food that swims, I tried some anyway because it was *his* choice.

We talked and laughed late into the night, having such a good time that we prolonged the date by stopping by my friend Kelly's Christmas party after dinner. While there, I noticed Bart's back pocket was ripped, revealing his underwear. Had it been anyone else, I might have been embarrassed. but with Bart it somehow seemed endearing. We drove home on the back roads, and when it came time to say good night, with his eyes gazing into mine, I felt an amazing calmness. As he leaned closer until his lips touched mine, it was like electricity shot throughout my body, triggering a feeling I had never experienced before, not a sexual feeling but a magical one only understandable to Bart and me.

Within a week we had begun seeing each other every day, even on

Christmas, which came only a few weeks after our first date. My gift to him that year became a joke between us as time passed. Since with other guys I had dated I had gone all out with a first gift and then felt too pushy, I tried to play it cool with Bart. Knowing that he disliked my love of country music and teased me when I would wake up with such songs in my head, I put together a tape of my favorite country songs. But when I opened his wonderful gifts to me, a beautiful long-sleeved shirt he had driven up to Bogus Basin Recreation Area to pick out because he knew I liked to ski and a bolo made at an Idaho rock store in downtown Boise, I knew I had struck a wrong note with my gift to him. Fortunately, over the years that followed I had many opportunities to make up for it.

During this period, we spent many a night out in Boise. Our favorite spot for dining and listening to music was the Lock, Stock & Barrel, voted our town's best steakhouse. On one night out together, I took Bart to the mall to show him the ring I loved, which I called "my ring." "You better get it fixed before you give it to me," I said jokingly.

Bart not only listened attentively when I talked about everything in my life, he also supported me in whatever daily challenge I faced. For example, one night, after I'd been fired from a job in escrow, he took me to the Bogus Basin Recreation Area, found a scenic spot with a view of the city, and popped a bottle of champagne in the car.

"What's this for?" I asked, perplexed about his actions implying something positive had happened that day.

"We're celebrating. You're finally out of that hell hole!" he replied.

In March we took our first road trip, which was to Lake Tahoe for the wedding of one of Bart's friends. After a night out with the wedding crowd, we went off by ourselves to a scenic, romantic spot. We were talking almost nonstop when I thought I heard Bart say, "I love you." So I immediately said, "Me too!"—just in case I had heard him incorrectly. A few minutes later we were wrapped in a tender embrace, kissing, when a security guard knocked on our window, making us laugh at the stereotypical situation. On the drive back to Boise, we stopped at a service station to buy a new tape, determined to find some music that we could enjoy together. We selected a Michael Bolton recording, and though others might have considered it sappy we loved it. One night soon after, Bart told me, "I never knew what real love was until I met you."

Early in the fall we had a date scheduled when Bart was uncharacteristically late coming to pick me up. I was hungry and also angry after his explanation that he had been delayed shopping for a new Land Cruiser didn't make sense, but we said no more about it. Then on November 11, we had plans to go to B. B. Strand's, but the day before, Bart called and asked if it was okay to have our date at the house. Although a bit disappointed not to be going back to the site of our first date, I agreed to go to what we called the "good house" because it was located on Good Street.

My disappointment immediately vanished when I walked in the front door to see the cream-colored Italian leather sofas had been pushed back to make room for a blanket in front of the fireplace; place settings had been meticulously laid out; candles had been lit, providing the only light in the living room; and wine glasses had been set close to the fire.

Bart had already cooked dinner, a chicken stir fry with rice, and although he gracefully moved the food from the kitchen to our fireside location he seemed mysteriously nervous. "I just thought this would be more romantic than going out tonight," he said, grinning while picking up his chopsticks.

I nodded. We talked animatedly as we always did during dinner. When we were finished, I got up to take the dishes to the kitchen.

"You're not going to do the dishes now, are you? You're coming right back, aren't you?" he asked.

"Yeah, I'm just putting them in the sink," I murmured, still wondering what was making him anxious. When I returned to the living room, the cause was immediately apparent. I was astonished to see he was wearing "my ring" on the pinky of his right hand.

"Look how it shines in the firelight," he stated casually.

Now *I* was the nervous one. I wrapped my arms around him and rocked back and forth for what seemed like at least a half hour.

"Does this mean yes?" he finally asked.

"Yes," I said clearly. "There is nothing I want more!"

Though it was only eleven months into our relationship, I knew that Bart and I were meant to be husband and wife—forever. And, sure enough, we planned our wedding for six months later, on May 8, 1993. Bart had the ring from JC Penney configured to be my wedding ring, and he did remember to fix the prongs!

There was only one place we could be married: The Beautiful Savior Lutheran Church. That's the place that had brought us together and where I realized we were destined to be together. Mom and Dad bought the wedding dress I had spotted, with tiny, elegant beads in front and sleeves with a slight poof that made me feel like a princess out of a fairy tale. The night before the wedding, when I was trying so hard to stay in control despite my nerves, I was facing toward the audience while rehearsing when suddenly the others in the wedding party began to laugh. It turned out that Bart was behind me, mimicking my gestures. He knew just what to do to bring me back to earth.

On the day of the wedding I didn't let Bart see me before the ceremony, and when I walked into church I heard him gasp. As his eyes welled up with tears, I sensed his pride. I guess I took his breath away, and he sure did that for me. A friend played the trumpet as my dad walked me down the aisle. My two sisters stood beside me while Bart's brother Todd and my brother Steve stood beside him. Jody Light read from the Book of Psalms, and Susan Cornwell's voice perfected the ceremony. Our brothers and sisters treated us to a limo ride to our reception, which was in the Crystal Ballroom in the Hoff Building. We made sure our first dance was to "Now That I Found You" by Michael Bolton. I would never forget that night, which seemed perfect in every way and such a powerful expression of our love. So many details of it, especially Bart's face, would flash back to haunt me after the accident.

Chapter 2
The Boys

RECOUNTING THE MOMENT Benjamin Joel Kraft entered the world on June 2, 1995 at 4:19 pm always brought Bart and me much joy, as well as much laughter. Because my blood pressure was extremely high, our doctor, Dr. Carter, decided to induce labor at 1:30 pm. Immediately after my water broke I had a contraction that seemed to last the full two hours and forty-nine minutes of the birth. I did receive an epidural but never felt the effects of it—only a lot of pain.

Bart and Mom were both in the hospital room. I asked Mom to be there because I wanted her to know how much she meant to me, how much a part of my life she was, and how much I appreciated everything she had done for me. Bart was there because I couldn't imagine him not being with me at such a meaningful time for both of us. Ironically, he almost missed the show!

After the epidural, Bart, assuming it was going to be a while before the delivery, decided he would go get a bottle of pop with my brother Steve. But as he stepped out of my room, Bart figured out that they'd have to walk to an entirely different floor of the hospital to find a drink. Not able to bear being that far from me, he instructed Steve to bring back a pop for him. Just as Bart reentered my room, he caught a glimpse of the baby's head emerging from my womb. "We're having a baby!" he screamed, loud enough for everyone on the floor to hear. Benjamin must have heard him, too, because he shot right out at that very moment. Luckily, Dr. Carter was there to catch him! All I saw was perfection. Benjamin was so beautiful.

As we settled into parenthood, Benjamin did everything right: slept through the night, took naps during the day, ate on schedule. We could not have asked for an easier baby. Of course, Bart and I were still exhausted, and we definitely felt the loss of freedom, independence, and control that come with starting a family. Yet, the good outweighed the bad by a couple of tons. Laughter and love filled all our waking and half-sleeping moments.

It didn't take long to discover that Benjamin was extremely smart. He spoke in full sentences practically from the moment he was born—at least that's the way I remember it. I vividly recall one morning when we were at the breakfast table and Benjamin, eighteen months old, said angrily, "You make me nervous, Mamma!"

"Well, Benjamin," I replied, calmly, "when you figure out what nervous means then I will let you talk that way." I didn't let him know how impressed I was by his verbal prowess.

By age two, he would lie in front of the stereo speaker, listen to the entire sound track of *Phantom of the Opera*, and explain to me in great detail what the characters were feeling while they were singing. When we'd take him to the amusement park, he would study the rides with such a serious expression that some people with us wondered if he was really having fun. Then, on the car ride home, he would excitedly explain exactly how each ride worked. Yes, my son was going to be a deep thinker and a sensitive soul.

Samuel Garfield Kraft arrived on September 12, 1997, as a bright burst of energy! From then on, when Samuel entered a room, everyone noticed, as every ounce of him oozed the joy of living his childhood fully. From the time he was born, Samuel never wanted to miss anything, which naturally made it a bit difficult for me to keep up with him. Since Benjamin was less this way, I came to appreciate very early what a blessing it was to have one calm, intellectual child and one creative but extremely active child. Despite Samuel's activity, I held my own, with lots of help from Bart and my mom.

Another helpful thing was that Benjamin, who was a bit older than two when Samuel was born, was still taking three- to four-hour naps in the afternoon, even though Samuel might nap for only fifteen minutes in the morning and another fifteen minutes in the afternoon. Consequently, I didn't have to keep up with both of them all the time, although sometimes it seemed that way. I especially remember one night of utter exhaustion when the boys kept waking each other up. When I would finally get Samuel asleep, Benjamin would call out, "Mommy, don't forget me!" The only one in the house getting any sleep was Bart, and I decided I had to let him know about that. Grabbing a pillow, I woke my husband by hitting him over the head a few times, shouting, "It's your turn!" Finally Bart, at last, rose to the occasion.

Benjamin was also always looking for ways to help me with Samuel. I only breast-fed Samuel for a month, and in the ensuing months Benjamin eagerly volunteered to hold the bottle for many a feeding. He also would get me wipes and even clean Samuel while I watched over him. I always let him know how much I appreciated his help, and even when I was feeling impatient or we were running late for something I tried to resist the urge to take control. That choice reaped dividends, because my two boys soon became inseparable and hardly ever fought. In fact, by the time Samuel was two, Bart and I could see that they were such "buds" they wanted to be together all the time. So although they had separate bedrooms they began sleeping together. Watching them when they had peacefully drifted off to the world of dreams filled me with awe.

Mom embraced her role as grandmother. "I love my kids, but my grandbabies are my life," she would say, and she would show it at every turn. When the boys were young, she would stay with me to help with them all day, then respectfully slip out before Bart came home to give us time together. At Christmas she hosted a cookie decorating party for all her grandchildren and their friends, which evolved into a wondrous mess.

In our times together watching the boys, Mom often confided in me about her own life issues. We talked about how she had stayed in Weiser after the divorce so my brother Steve and I would have continuity in our teen years, and so she could continue to date Dick. Now she was thriving in Boise because she was, at heart, a city girl. After never having had a job outside the home before her divorce, she was enjoying her work as a real estate agent. Of course, she still had her own struggles, and I felt so grateful that when she chose to confide in me I could be of some comfort to her, just as she had always been for me.

"So when are you two going to cut the cord?" Dick would ask about Mom and I. The unspoken answer was "hopefully never."

My dad also loved spending time with his grandsons, and it was always nice to see that he and Mom graciously accepted being together for important family occasions. Duane and LaVonne, Bart's parents, lived in Tacoma but were very much a part of our family, too.

We went on many fun family outings. One I particularly remember was a trip to California in June 2000 so Bart and his brother Todd could attend the one hundredth anniversary of the US Open. Bart had been at Pebble Beach in 1982 for one of the most famous moments in US Open history, when Tom Watson chipped in a shot from the rough and stormed to victory. After Bart and Todd had walked the fairways of Pebble Beach, we all met for dinner at Bubba Gump Shrimp Co. in Monterey. When Bart and I had previously celebrated our fifth anniversary in Maui, I had pledged to stop at every Bubba Gump's during my lifetime.

It was a special time for Bart and Todd, and during this getaway Bart and I squeezed in a romantic return to Tahoe. Since we had brought Dad along to watch the boys, we were able to slip away to the same lookout spot where Bart had first said, "I love you." When we were kissing there and a security officer rapped on our car window just as had occurred in the past, we loved it.

Initially, Bart and I had lived in the same house on Good Street where he had proposed. When I drive by there today, I notice that it still has the same bench on the porch that once had been a church pew. When it was time to upgrade to a family home, we relied on Mom as our real estate agent to find the right place, and she located one that just happened to be a stone's throw from her home. No, that cord was not being cut, and we still maintained it when Mom and Dick finally got married. "I don't blame you for marrying her," I told Dick. "I can't live without her either."

My sister Jody lived in the same Elwood area, which meant I could spend time with my niece Sarah, who had a laugh that would light up a room. Sarah had come into our lives only weeks after Bart and I had married, and we were her godparents. After battling endometriosis, Jody and her husband Paul had decided to adopt, and we were all blessed by the arrival of this baby girl.

Our two families were very close, and our interactions led to many memorable events. When Sarah first learned to talk, she would not call me Aunt Jill but instead Puppy. She was a year old, and we had just gotten a Dalmatian puppy named Cinder—a wonderfully sweet, energetic dog that Sarah loved being near. Being called Puppy disturbed me at first, so I was relieved when eventually Sarah began calling me Aunt Jill. But now I see how calling me Puppy was Sarah's way of bestowing honor and affection.

One day while the boys and I were visiting Jody and Sarah, Samuel fed Sarah's fish Starlight the whole bottle of fish food, for the umpteenth time. To hold him accountable, Jody told Samuel to put his nose against the wall, which he regarded as an act of torture. "Aunt Dody, I on't tink tis is a berry good idea," he said. But I thought it was a great move. From that day on, I had a punishment that got through to Samuel.

When Samuel was three, Bart and I decided to build a larger house in which to raise our boys, one that wouldn't seem too small even when they were teenagers. Since we both enjoyed golf, we also wanted to be close to a good golf course. An added bonus would be to find a suitable home close to Bart's brother Todd, who lived outside Boise in Eagle. We had been spending so much time with my family that we both liked the idea of becoming more a part of Todd and Lisa's family and having more time with my niece Joanna and my nephew Brian. Bart loved and admired his brother, and the stories he told about their deep friendship during childhood reminded me of Benjamin and Samuel's relationship.

Bart was hoping to buy an existing house, but the one we wanted was sold before we could act. So we decided to build our house, and we were fortunate to wind up with the best builder ever: Peter Harris at Harris Homes. Peter built us a wonderful home, and along the way we all became friends. The boys, especially Samuel, would get excited whenever "Mr. Peter" dropped by. When the house was finished, Peter told us he was bringing his wife Clissa over so we could meet her. Unfortunately, Samuel got a little too excited this time. When his hyper behavior made it impossible for us to talk, I put him in time-out on the steps. Later I counted to ten in my bedroom and came out to discuss what had happened.

"Samuel, do you understand how badly you just behaved?" I asked, looking frustrated at him.

"Who let the dogs out?" he replied. That was the title of a hit song at the time, but I had no idea where Samuel could have heard it as we didn't listen to the radio and I had never heard the boys singing it. In response, all I could say was, "Huh?" as I tried to conceal a grin. Life with our boys was full of funny, touching, memorable moments.

Once we moved into our dream house, we were living near Boise, a city that felt completely like home to both Bart and me, even though neither of us had grown up there. We were surrounded by our loving and caring families. Bart had an excellent job, and I had found the life direction that Mom had predicted I would discover someday: to be a loving wife and dedicated mother. I could see no reason why that would ever change.

Chapter 3
The Once-in-a-Lifetime Opportunity

OCTOBER 2000 WAS A BUSY TIME for the Kraft family. Bart's job at Micron sometimes required him to travel to Japan and Singapore, and although we always loved the beautiful presents he brought back it was difficult to have him away. Benjamin was doing well his first year in kindergarten, and Samuel was a whirlwind at home. When I wasn't scurrying around to keep up with him, I focused on my other major job: getting settled in the new house. Mom was my project manager. When she showed up to help, she would set a goal for the day, saying something like, "Okay, Jill, we're going to get rid of four boxes today," and she would make sure we met our goal.

That year we enjoyed our first Christmas in the Eagle home, and amid all the chaos of wrapping presents and cooking and the buzz of extended family visits and Christmas music, I found a few peaceful moments to simply appreciate what a wonderful life we were creating together as a family.

Then came the job offer. Bart and I were in our bedroom after the boys had gone to bed when he announced, "Jill, Wayne called. He was at the Hard Rock Café in London. He told me about the amazing experience he was having. He wondered why we weren't there having a drink with him."

I tugged nervously at a pillow, sensing where this conversation might be going. Micron had been doing more and more overseas work and calling upon some of their most trusted people in their Boise office to work overseas. Wayne had known Bart for years and valued him highly as a bright, talented engineer and administrator.

"Wayne would really like me to work for a year at our plant in Italy," Bart continued. "He said it would be a great cultural experience for our family. I think so, too."

I never wanted to let Bart down or hold him back from something he wanted to do, but "great cultural experience" in a distant country was far from my ideal vision of our shared life. As far as I was concerned, we were busy raising a family, and there was plenty of culture in Boise. And what guarantee could Bart give me that everything would be okay over there? I wondered.

"Are you sure this is something you want us to seriously consider?" I asked. "Benjamin will be in first grade in the fall. Samuel will be starting preschool. Think of how hard it would be to uproot them."

"The boys will be fine. We'll help them," said Bart. He moved closer, looked me in the eyes, and added, "Jill, this is a once-in-a-lifetime opportunity. There's so much to see and do in Italy—so much beauty and history and architecture. I hear the food is terrific, and we both like Italian dishes. How can we pass this up? It would only be for a year."

I touched Bart's cheek for a second. When you love a man as deeply as I loved Bart, and you're looking into his eyes, saying no seems impossible. "Well, if you're sure this is something you want to do, you know I will support you," I said, managing a faint smile. "But I have just one question: how the heck am I going to get over there?"

I had recently become afflicted by a fear of flying. A couple of weeks before Christmas that year Bart and I had decided we'd get away for some sightseeing and Christmas shopping in New York. While Mom took care of the boys, we enjoyed a relaxing, romantic time—until the flight back from New York to Denver. I had a sudden panic attack and couldn't stop shaking and crying. At one point Bart took out the magnetic Scrabble game we had brought for the trip and said, "Come on, Jill, focus on this." But it didn't work. Neither did the flight attendant's best efforts to calm me down. I was a basket case until we safely touched the ground.

I hadn't always been afraid to fly. I had aced the test of flying to Hawaii for our fifth anniversary excursion. But for that trip I hadn't needed to fly in or out of Denver, a prime hub for Boise flights that I associated with bad memories of an airline accident. While in college, I had walked into the dorm room and heard one of my girlfriends shout hysterically, "There was an accident in Denver—the plane broke in half. And my parents were on that plane!" Her mom and dad had been among the twenty-eight casualties on a Continental flight bound for Boise that had crashed on takeoff at Denver's Stapleton Airport because it had not been properly deiced.

"We'll get you help for your fear of flying," Bart said. "We'll ask our doctor to do something for you. Tell you what. You and I will go over by ourselves for a week, just to check things out. Then we can decide, okay?"

"Just to check it out?" I repeated. "And if it doesn't feel right, I can say no?"

Bart nodded and wrapped his arms around me, but it sure didn't feel like the hug in front of his fireplace when he asked me to marry him. This was a different kind of invitation, one that wasn't part of my dream. But, I understood, it was part of marital give-and-take.

So, though I never cared much for medication of any kind, I medicated myself up the wazoo and got on the plane to Italy. I don't remember much about the flight, except giggling a lot and acting spacy. At one point Bart looked at me, shook his head, and said, "Looks like I'm going to be taking three kids to Italy when we go as a family."

After our arrival in Italy, one of our first sights at the Rome airport was of eight Carabinieri—Italy's military police—with Uzis, surrounding a man no more than twenty yards from us, but fortunately the nice-looking Italian man who met us was more welcoming! Soon we were in his black Mercedes making the hour and a half drive to Avezzano, located in the Abruzzo region of central Italy. There he dropped us off at Micron's semiconductor plant, which the company had bought a few years earlier. As I shook off my medication haze, I thought about what I needed to say to Wayne. I knew he had a reputation for wanting employees to work long hours, showing up for work at 6:00 or 7:00 am and staying until 8:00 pm. Bart was going to have an important role as a fabrications manager, so much would be expected of him. And I knew how competitive Bart could be in the work environment. He would naturally feel he had to keep up with Wayne's expectations.

During lunch at the plant, I pulled Wayne aside and told him, "I know how much Bart wants to come and how much you want him here, but you understand that the boys and I come first for Bart when he's here, right?"

"Of course," he replied, laughing. "Bart just needs to give us one hundred percent during the days, and weekends now and then, and we will make sure you and your family have a great experience here."

I nodded, not entirely convinced, and Wayne continued his tour.

Not long after lunch I was zonked out in our hotel room trying to recover from the change in time zones when I awoke to a loud buzzing noise coming from the bathroom.

"Bart, are you okay?" I shouted. "What's that noise?"

"I just pulled this cord in the shower," he explained. "Maybe it's some kind of alarm."

The desk clerk later confirmed Bart's guess. "Don't worry," he said. "Most Americans pull that cord on their first visit."

While Bart headed off for an orientation day at the Micron plant, I checked the offerings on TV. Immediately I saw a rather explicit sexual situation being shown. Red flag! At home, I already limited TV for the boys, but it looked like it was going to be no TV at all in Italy. A few minutes later I got a phone call from Deborah, one of the wives of the Micron contingent from Boise, asking me if I was hungry.

"Starving," I said.

"I'll take you to one of the bars nearby," she said.

A bar in the morning? Did she think I wanted a drink? I wondered. It turned out to be another educational experience to discover that bars in Italy are closer to our cafés or coffee shops, though they do serve liquor. Deborah recommended that I try the blood orange juice, and it was wonderful. In terms of food, Deborah pointed out that while the bar mostly served little cookies I could get a piece of toast or even a bowl of cereal, though the milk might taste a little funny. I wasn't really noticing the food as much as the clientele and method of service. This was no Starbucks where you stood in a clearly defined line, gave your order, and sat at a private table. The only way Deborah could even place our order was to shove her way to the front, and instead of sitting at a quiet table we stood huddling in a crowded corner to eat. "You'll get used to it," she said with a grin.

That evening Wayne insisted on taking us to one of the favorite restaurants of the Boise folks, about ten miles away in Tagliacozzo. We parked in the town's central square and walked through a dark alleyway until Wayne pointed to a small building with no sign. We walked inside a cold, open area with a cement floor and a few tables. A stout, grandmotherly looking woman stepped out of the back kitchen, where I could glimpse huge pots of boiling water. Explaining that they didn't use menus, Wayne ordered for us big plates of various pasta and sauces, with a wide selection of meats and cheeses, along with wine. All the food was delightful, as was the wine. I found the gnocchi tasty, and the fresh parmesan our hostess had made herself was superb.

At the end of the meal, Wayne urged us to try Grappa, an after-dinner drink made from grape skins. I didn't much care for it, but Bart enjoyed it because he's a scotch drinker and it had real strength, almost like fuel. It all made for an amazing experience, though I wasn't used to spending four hours over dinner! "Okay," I said to myself on the way home, "Italy appears to have its high points."

Over the next few days, while we continued to wake up in the middle of the night and I frequently checked the clock to imagine what the boys and Grandma were doing back home, I could see Bart overflowing with excitement. My husband loved new things and relished tasting the full experience of life. "Can you believe how nice these people are here?" he would say. "Look at the beauty of this country. We'll have so much to see with the boys. And can you believe the food, and how much of it they bring you?"

I would smile and look around, lost in other thoughts. Before I became convinced that we should move here I wanted some of the other expats and their wives to tell me more about the real difficulties in adjusting to living in Italy, to walk me through the potential land mines. Unfortunately, most of them had been here for several months or were getting ready to go back home, having done all their adjusting, so I was left to imagine the obstacles, and I was prone to distorting the picture somewhat. A couple of days before the end of our scouting trip I knew it was time to share my concerns with Bart since communication was highly valued in our marriage.

"I just keep thinking how we're going to be away from my mom and dad and how hard it will be for me to do all of this on my own," I began.

"I know you'll miss them," Bart said, "but think of it this way. We'll have time for just the four of us. At home there's always something going on with our families, but here it will be just us. Think of the closeness we will have."

Well, he had struck a high note there. It was true that I would often be pulled in many different directions at home. Being farther than a walk around the corner or a short drive from family would be different but perhaps have family benefits.

"Yes, but you're still going to be at work so much of the time, and I'll have so much to figure out on my own. And Wayne is really driven. You're going to have to put your foot down with him all the time. I can't have you come home at 8:00 or 9:00 every night, leave at 6:00 or 7:00 in the morning, and be at work again on weekends. If you're imagining anything like that, you're with the wrong person. You chose me, and you chose the boys. You have to put us first!" I said. I remembered how Wayne had reassured me that he understood our priorities, but I knew it was going to be up to Bart to hold him to it.

Bart held my shoulder gently, knowing me well enough to realize that I just needed to express my insecurities. "I will tell Wayne," he said firmly. "I'll be home for dinner every night, work weekends only occasionally, and I'll get time off for us to explore the country, especially when your family comes to visit. Remember, part of why I want to do this is because at home everyone gets a part of you: your dad, your mom, your brothers and sisters. Over here I will have you all to myself!"

What could I say to that? Bart always was a good deal-closer. Anyway, the reality was that since Micron had brought us over to Italy to scout things out we would have needed a major reason to tell them we weren't coming back. I just had to make sure there was nothing I could see that would hurt the boys or undermine our life together as a family, though I knew there could be no absolute reassurances.

On our final day, I agreed to do the "Rome speed tour," taking in everything we could in this ancient city in the seven hours we had to sightsee. We saw the Colosseum, the Vatican, the Pantheon, Michelangelo's *Moses*, and the Chains of St. Peter. I especially enjoyed the Chains of St Peter because it was off the tourist trail. At the Pantheon, I remembered how Bart had wanted to be an architect until high school when he realized there was no money in it unless you were famous. I imagined seeing more of the beauty of Italy's art and architecture through my husband's eyes if we moved to Italy.

After loading up on fun presents for the boys, including chocolate eggs with prizes inside, we left Italy. I again needed to be medicated before getting on the plane, but I wasn't nearly as anxious as I had been on the flight over. Once I make my mind up about something, I will stick to it. And I had made up my mind: I was taking my family to Italy.

Chapter 4
The Premonition

ONCE WE HAD MADE THE COMMITMENT to move to Italy for a year, Mom and I had a new project: organizing and packing for living in another country. Mom created categories of concerns on which to focus, such as schools in Italy, which I called Mom's Italy Checklist. And we strategized about how to deal with each concern. With the housing allowance from Micron, we would not need to take large items such as furniture. Micron maintained a warehouse of things left by other families who had returned from overseas assignments, so we could select some items there to further reduce our shopping in Italy. Also there was a weight limit to what we could bring over, so we had to carefully prioritize what we really needed and wanted. We had to move fast in order to to ship things over several weeks before we were due to depart in June.

The Micron families in Italy had told us, "You'll want to bring things with sentimental value that help you feel connected to home." We took this advice to heart. For our eighth anniversary, on May 8, Bart and I purchased a beautiful painting of Boise to take with us. And we knew that the boys would want to take their favorite toys to keep them occupied as well as their most treasured stuffed animals: Bear for Benjamin and Barkley for Samuel.

"And make sure they have pictures of everyone in the family with them," Mom suggested. So we chose the best photos of their cousins: Jack, my brother Steve and his wife Mary's son; Sarah, Jody and Paul's daughter; Michael, Spencer, and James, my sister Sue and her husband Rusty's boys; and Joanna and Brian, Uncle Todd and Aunt Lisa's older kids. And, of course, we pulled together a lively photo display of their grandparents.

For myself, Bart urged me to take the pottery wheel he had bought me on Valentine's Day that year, after which I'd begun taking ceramics classes.

"This will give you a chance to continue to develop your passion, and you'll have a good opportunity to learn all about the art in Italy," he said. I was enthusiastic about the idea of further participating in pottery making in a country with a history of artistic excellence.

Before leaving we enjoyed one last family excursion. Bart's parents were celebrating their fortieth anniversary that May, and since they lived near Seattle we decided the entire family would celebrate together on nearby Orcas Island after a party in Tacoma. Remembering how much Dad had enjoyed the limo we got for his seventieth birthday, Todd and Bart arranged a surprise limo for Duane and LaVonne, which was a big hit.

Both boys were excited about going to Italy. To help prepare them, Bart went around the house putting up little stickers with the Italian word for objects they would see every day: *tavolo* for table; *frigorifero* for refrigerator; *della luce* for light switch. Benjamin kept telling everyone that this was only going to be his first of many adventures in different countries. Unlike his mom, he loved flying. One day he told us that when he grew up he would be a dad with five kids and be the copilot with his cousin Jack on Peanut Butter Airlines. Samuel, who was not yet four years old, didn't understand as much about what was happening. He was having fun with the talk about a new place that would be our home, yet at the same time I could tell he was nervous about leaving his comfort zone. For both boys, leaving Grandma, Sarah, and everyone else was going to be difficult. Samuel kept telling me how much he was going to miss Starlight, Sarah's fish. "Who's going to make sure Starlight has enough to eat?" he kept saying.

Taking care of our new house in Eagle was not going to be a problem since I had my friends Kari and Luke lined up for house and dog sitting. We just had one little complication with the timing of our departure: Benjamin's sixth birthday was on June 2, the day before we were to leave for Italy, and obviously we had to make time to celebrate it. With the timing, we decided the event would be a combination of Benjamin's birthday party and our family's going-away party.

Benjamin was allowed to select the theme for his birthday party, as he did every year. We wondered what it would be as he sometimes had eccentric tastes. I remembered how, when we got him a drawing book, I asked him what his favorite color was and he replied, "Magenta." And when instructed to draw his favorite person, he drew his friend Laura, the daughter of my friend Martha, explaining, "I've asked Laura to marry me." Ultimately, Benjamin asked to have the party at Roaring Springs, a water park outside of Boise. He was especially eager to see Doby the Dolphin, the park's mascot. "I want to talk to him, Mamma," he said. On the day of his birthday party Benjamin insisted on following Doby around, and as I watched him hugging the dolphin and beaming, I was reminded of how Benjamin saw happiness and love in almost everything. The world, to him, was indeed a beautiful place.

After the fun and frolicking at Roaring Springs, the family all gathered at our house. Dad was the first to head home that evening, and since he lived an hour away and would not be with the contingent sending us off at the Boise airport the next morning, we had to say good-bye then.

"This is even harder than I thought it would be, Dad," I said as I began to tear up.

"Oh, honey, it's a piece of cake for me," he said, then he jumped in his car and drove off fast so I could barely see him crying.

"I am never going to see Dad again," I said, as I looked into Mom's eyes.

"What?" she said. "Your father is not going to die."

"I know that. It's just that…he won't ever be…my dad again," I explained, not understanding myself why I was speaking in such an ominous way.

This was the first moment of having what I would call an inner knowing, or premonition, about the outcome of our trip to Italy. I sensed that something, whether good or bad, was going to happen to loved ones, however improbable it may have seemed to others at the time.

I had a history of experiencing premonitions about events, which, unfortunately sometimes occurred as I had foreseen. Soon after Benjamin was born I had felt compelled to write a note for him to read in case something happened to me. "Every day that I leave you, I worry that something will happen to me or to you and we may never see each other again," it began. The note went on to tell him some of the things I would want him to know if I died when he was still young. When Samuel was born, I added my personal thoughts for him to the note. My note included references to my hope that my boys would continue to know God in their lives, because one of my biggest fears was that if I died they could lose faith in God. I kept the letter in my underwear drawer, figuring that no one would be apt to stumble upon it while I was around but no one could miss finding it if I died. I told Bart it was there, but he never read it.

I can't say that I knew anything specific would happen when I wrote this note for the boys, because I simply felt that if anything ever did happen to me I would want to have left a message to comfort Benjamin and Samuel. It gave me peace of mind knowing the note was there.

Feeling a sense that something was going to happen could be a very positive thing at times. After all, when I first laid eyes on Bart at the church singles' event I knew this was the man I would marry. When I was much younger, I had had the same feeling about Kelly when I first came across her in elementary school. "Mom, I don't know what it is, but I feel like Kelly is going to be a big part of my life," I said one day. I remember one of those writing exercises in school where you're asked what you would do if you had a million dollars, and I answered that I would build Kelly her dream home up in the mountains where she would be surrounded by nature's beauty. Today, Kelly is still a prominent part of my life, as she has been through it all. So I was totally right about Bart and Kelly.

In addition, many times I have experienced waking up in the middle of the night knowing that someone close to me was hurting, only to discover later that a friend had lost someone close to them that very night. I had had such premonitions about Bart a couple of times, too. For example, when I bought him a paper tree and it died after only a year and a half I took that as a sign that maybe we weren't going to be together forever after all. Then, on our seventh anniversary, while we were making a toast with champagne, Bart's glass broke, which I also interpreted as an ominous indication for his life.

I managed to shake off the premonition about Dad enough to get through the last night at home, but at the airport the next morning, I experienced an even stronger premonition that went beyond Dad and encompassed my entire family. Mom and Dick, along with Jody and her family, and Steve and his family, all came to see us off at the gate. I had taken my medication, so my fear of flying had diminished. But suddenly something else caused me anxiety. As we got closer and closer to the gate, I became shaky and began crying, just sobs initially and then hysterical bawling.

"Jill, what is it?" Mom finally asked.

"I can't go! I can't do it!" I shrieked. "I'm not going to come home with them. I'm not going to come home with them!"

Mom and Jody wrapped their arms around me and reassured me, but I wasn't able to listen to them. All I could hear was my inner knowing, my premonition that something bad would happen. I didn't want to feel that way. I was a wife and mother who had agreed to go along to Italy for this once-in-a-lifetime adventure. I didn't want to put a damper on this exciting moment for everybody. In the days leading up to our departure, I had experienced enthusiasm and anticipation; but now a premonition persisted that somehow my family would not be with me here in Boise again. How, when, why—I didn't know, but the feeling was overwhelming.

Finally, as Mom and Jody kept the boys occupied Bart pulled me aside and said firmly but calmly, "Jill, you need to stop this now. You're thinking morbidly. Everything's going to be okay. And you know that God would never give you anything you can't handle."

For the sake of my family, I needed to believe that everything would be okay in Italy. Otherwise, I'd be a nervous wreck the whole time we were there and ruin this chance for such a special closeness. So I tried very hard to believe that everything was going to be okay, so hard that I convinced myself I really did believe it.

Chapter 5
First Taste of Italy

FROM THE FIRST WEEKEND WE WERE IN ITALY, Bart, Benjamin, Samuel, and I began exploring different areas of the country. Our first overnight excursion was to Sorrento, a famous tourist town in southern Italy overlooking the Bay of Naples. The view from our hotel was so expansive you could see not only Naples but Mt. Vesuvius. We were told that Luciano Pavarotti loved to vacation there, and we could see why.

Bart had somehow found us a room at the Bellevue Syrene, which we were told was quite a feat since everything was booked well in advance around there in June and July. When we first got to our hotel room, the boys and I raced to the minibar to pick out a treat and a drink. This became a tradition after checking into hotels, and although Bart never quite understood our enjoyment of it he eventually joined in. Benjamin and Samuel soon immersed themselves in the beautiful pool and then insisted that we walk the five hundred steps down to the beach. After some shopping and dinner in town, Bart and I got the boys in a warm bath and made them a bed together on the floor. Benjamin had Bear with him, and Samuel was hugging Barkley. Those two bears that Mom had gotten for them when they were born would go everywhere with our boys. Per our usual bedtime routine, Bart read them two stories, and I sang to them. They fell asleep, arms wrapped around each other.

Now it was time for Bart and me to enjoy the terrace. Bart poured us each a warm cognac and put them down on the mosaic table. Knowing it was still afternoon back home, we called Mom to tell her how incredible the view was. As we sipped our drinks and gazed out into the distance, we suddenly were treated to a display of fireworks near Mt. Vesuvius.

"Amazing, isn't it?" Bart asked.

I glanced from the glittering fireworks, to the sea lit up below, to the face of the man I loved. It was a romantic moment, almost surreal. "I don't know if I've ever seen anything more beautiful in my life," I said finally. "Can you believe that we're really here, doing this?"

"I told you it would be an experience we couldn't pass up," Bart said with a smile. I felt so in love with him, with my family, with the possibilities of this new life.

The next morning we drove along the legendary Amalfi Coast, where village after village is built along the high cliffs above the bright blue waters of the Mediterranean. We stopped for lunch in Positano, a town known for the production of Limoncello, a popular liqueur made out of the lemon rinds from lemons grown on terraced gardens along the coast. Scenes from such movies as *Under the Tuscan Sun* were filmed along this coast, which took my breath away. Almost from the start Positano emerged as our favorite getaway location. During our first stay there Bart approached me after checking out an art studio halfway down to the village while I was trying to entertain Benjamin and Samuel. Eyes beaming, he told me he had found an artwork we couldn't live without and guided me back there. When we entered the studio it looked like one anywhere, but then when we walked upstairs and Bart opened the door to the roof of the building, there was an additional display of beautiful art. Bart showed me the work of the artist he especially admired: Antonio Di Viccaro. Since it was just the beginning of our stay in Italy, I told Bart that if, by the following summer, we still thought this was the artist whose artwork we wanted, we would come back and buy something. It was a promise I would not forget. So within just a few weeks of our arrival in Italy, I was appreciating the beauty of this ancient country that was now our home.

Soon we got to see much more of the country. We discovered Pescara, a larger city along the Adriatic Coast with a history predating the Roman conquest. The boys loved the beach, and we quickly caught on to the Italian way of renting a beach spot with chairs, learning that most Italians rent them for designated days or weeks throughout the summer.

Another early favorite side trip was to Orvieto in southwestern Italy, a city that rises above tuft cliffs. A labyrinth of underground caves and tunnels attracts historians from around the world, and Bart wasted no time descending into a well to explore. Nearby, we liked the smaller town of Todi on the bank of the river Tiber, where I found some great deals on pottery and bought a cutting board of olive wood. Benjamin and Samuel bought whistles made from clay painted in the form of an elephant and a fish. We stayed in a hotel between Orvieto and Todi. I had my doubts about it initially because it was only a three-star hotel, but it turned out to be magnificent, with a picture-perfect view of a lake. While the boys slept inside, Bart and I played Pictionary outside the room. It was a humid July evening, but with the breeze blowing, the leaves rustling, the moon shining, the stars out, the sweet smell of flowers, and only occasional laughter in the distance disturbing the silence we were treated to another magical moment.

The diverse and distinctive architecture of the palaces and churches of Todi captured Bart's eye, but Samuel liked the town for a different reason. "Jody lives in Todi," he would say over and over again, connecting the sound of the town's name to his aunt back home in Boise. This would become a running joke in our family for the next several months.

In early July, only a month after we got to Italy, Bart and I, along with our friends Jonathan and Sheri, and Max and Cay from Micron, obtained tickets for a Sting concert at the soccer arena in Rome. Our seats were no more than thirty yards from the stage, and, with other friends watching the boys at home, we thoroughly enjoyed a special night out.

Closer to home, in the Abruzzo province where Avezzano was located, Micron organized outings to such sites as Rocca Calascio, a mountaintop fortress where the movie *Ladyhawke* with Michelle Pfeiffer and Matthew Broderick was filmed, and San Benedetto dei Marsi, known for its underground road and ruins. I was more interested in a visit to Caserta, a town at the foot of a mountain range where we learned how silk was made. The silk sold for $500 a yard! Benjamin picked out some less expensive fabric to make a pillow for Grandma LaVonne. Before we left town, we toured the Royal Palace of Caserta, a Baroque structure with painted ceilings that Mozart was said to enjoy.

With so many wondrous sights and such fascinating history to absorb, sometimes we felt like we were on an extended vacation. But my focus first and foremost remained on creating a comfortable and enjoyable family life in a place far from Boise. And that part of the Italy experience was not always so easy and pretty.

The challenges of everyday life in Italy had begun with finding a suitable place to live. Micron initially set us up in a small apartment in Celano, about twenty minutes from Avezzano. Soon after arriving in Italy we were directed to follow a woman there, and as she drove like a bat out of hell Bart quipped, "I don't think I can keep up with her." My head spun as I watched how fast-moving cars and pedestrians zigzagged around each other with no apparent organization, thinking that the pace could result in accidents. When we entered the furnished place, I glanced around at all the easily breakable crystal and the elegant grand piano.

"How is Samuel supposed to spend each day around all this without breaking or damaging things?" I mumbled, flashing on to images of my always lovable but often wild young boy tearing through the place and leaving it in shambles.

About 6:00 pm, as we wondered what our dinner options might be we got a call from Jonathan and Sheri, whom we had known through our church in Boise before Jonathan had been transferred to Italy ahead of Bart. They invited us to their place so we could go out for pizza, and we found them in an apartment complex more centrally located in Avezzano. As I noticed all the shops and restaurants nearby, I wondered if we also could be in such a place.

Later that night when the boys had settled in I said to Bart, "This place they assigned us is not going to work out. You're going to be gone all day, and it will be a half-hour drive for me to get anywhere I need to go. I'd like to have everything within walking distance. Can't you get us moved into that apartment complex where Jonathan and Sheri live?"

"I can try," he said, "but you realize that would be only a transitional place. We would need to find another home within a couple of months."

"We'll worry about that later," I said. "We need something better than this right now."

Eventually, the people at Micron did move us into the apartment complex. Our family of four, which had just been getting used to a 3,500-square-foot house near Boise, was now going to be taking up quarters in a 500-square-foot apartment. The entire kitchen was about as big as our dining table back home, so the boys couldn't even be in there with me while I was fixing meals. The only sleeping arrangement we could figure out was to take the top mattress off the bed in the one bedroom and move it into the living room at 8:00 each night. Bart and I slept on that, while the boys slept together on the bottom part of the bed in the bedroom. It became kind of comical: Mom and Dad having to make their bed at night in the boys' play area. This was going to be another adjustment to living in a foreign country. But we couldn't complain. After all, we had wanted to be closer as a family!

We found a day-care center for Benjamin and Samuel for times when I took Italian lessons or went out for lunch or other brief outings with expats. No one spoke English there, which Benjamin didn't seem to mind. He had already learned some Spanish and was looking forward to adding Italian to his repertoire. For Samuel, the scene was more intimidating, especially when the young women attendants would come right up to me as we walked in and literally tear him out of my arms. As always, Benjamin was there to help his little brother, reading to him or just reassuring him that he would be all right in this new hangout. Benjamin also enjoyed "all the pretty girls," as he described the teenagers who were part of the staff there.

Around home, Samuel was certainly making himself known among the other Micron families in the apartment complex. I remember the time we had a rare evening out, leaving the children with a sitter to attend a going-away party for Max and Cay, who lived on the seventh floor, above our third-floor unit. We left for the party before Max and Cay, and soon after they arrived, they whispered to Bart about something that had happened at our apartment, making him howl with laughter.

"What is it?" I asked him when he came back over to me, and, laughing, he told me that apparently, as Max and Cay had arrived at the apartment complex, the boys ran out on the deck to greet them. Max said to Samuel, "Hey, Squirt!" Samuel didn't like being called anything other than Samuel, and especially not Squirt. To show his displeasure, he said, "I not Squirt, I Samuel" as he whipped around, pulling his pants down to moon the couple. The story wasn't so funny to me because Samuel had been making a habit of such displays around us, and while Benjamin and Bart would often laugh and egg him on I had told them they should ignore Samuel and he would stop. In any case, Samuel was never dull!

As the mom in the house, I also needed to rise to the challenge of preparing food for my family in a place where I was not familiar with the markets or products. It was at times hard to get some foods fresh. Eggs were extremely difficult to get fresh. For example, during one visit to Tagliacozzo, a merchant took to the boys and wound up giving Benjamin an egg, puzzling him. "Mamma, why would that man give me an egg?" Benjamin asked. "Benjamin, fresh eggs are very precious here. He meant it as a nice gift." So Benjamin immediately ran over to the man and thanked him with a big hug.

Also, milk sold at local stores was not fresh and didn't taste very good. This presented a big change for two young boys who, back home in Boise, would consume a gallon and a half of milk in less than two days. But the boys soon got used to breakfasts of cereal and yogurt, or sometimes oatmeal or pancakes. I became as creative as I could with dinner, trying to give the boys enough of what they were used to while taking advantage of the new foods Italy had to offer them. We certainly had our fair share of pizza. I would make chicken, too, but had to accept Sheri's offer to buy the chickens for me at the grocer's because they were sometimes sold with the head still on, a local custom for which I was not ready.

I soon learned I could grow basil, rosemary, sage, and thyme in herb pots on the deck, so I made lots of soups as well. I mastered an Italian soup with chicken, herbs, crushed pepper, and stewed tomatoes. I'd often put tortellini or other small pastas in my soups, which the boys loved because the pasta was sold in many fun and unusual shapes. A soup with fresh, locally made parmesan cheese sprinkled on top, with fresh Italian bread on the side, was a very popular meal. Of course, I made lots of other basic pasta dishes, and I certainly appreciated the superior quality and freshness of the pasta compared with what I could buy in US supermarkets.

Vegetables were in abundant supply, especially since we arrived in early summer, but I had to get used to the Italian rule that it is prohibited to touch any vegetable at a store without first putting on the gloves that they provide. If you so much as try to touch them without gloves, someone will slap you on the wrist. It was hard to keep two very curious American boys from grabbing! For those times when I wanted something different, I would visit the "Uncle Ben's section" of our primary store, where international foods were stocked, and scoop up items like tortillas and salsa for taco salads.

I developed a fondness for the local olives. I loved spreading green olive cream cheese on Velva toast. For lunch I'd often make caprese, a basic summer salad with tomato, basil, and fresh mozzarella. I would also freeze lemon-lime soda in a small cake pan for margaritas. Almost every day we had to grocery shop, whether because of limited storage or our inability to avoid food spoilage—the price one pays for extremely fresh, preservative-free foods in a foreign country!

On evenings when the four of us would head out to the piazza for some local pizza, we soon discovered that we had to order by the slice because if we sat down and ordered a whole pizza it would usually mean a two- or three-hour wait. The boys quickly came to like an unusual twist on pizza often served in Italy: a topping of crisp potato resembling French fries. For a treat, we would also order gelato or hot chocolate, which was served in an espresso cup and had the consistency of pudding—the most amazing hot chocolate I had ever had!

Going to Fonte Rio quickly became a Friday night routine. All the Boise expats would meet there for a wonderful "family" meal if they weren't traveling or sightseeing. The boys loved it, especially when they finished their dinner and their friend Maximiliano would take them to grab a treat.

So it was clear from the start that I could put a solid check mark beside the "Food" category on my Mom's Italy Checklist. However, I couldn't yet check off the category of "Home" while living in the cramped, temporary apartment.

Fortunately, in August we took over the house that Brian, Wayne's boss at Micron, had been living in with his wife and children since Brian was going to be staying in Italy on his own for some time while his family returned to Boise. Suddenly, we had a three-story home with a spacious living room, dining room, kitchen, and three bedrooms. The upper floor was a loft that we quickly transformed into a playroom for the boys. They liked it so much they put up a sign that read: "Ben & Sam's Bedroom" because that's what they wanted it to be. They each had their own bedroom, which meant little to them since they still insisted on sleeping in the same room anyway. Benjamin, though, always found something special for "his" room with the $10 we gave each boy on our sightseeing trips. We also had a washer and dryer, a rarity for families in Italy, as well as a great deck and a yard in which the boys could play. We had definitely hit the Italy living jackpot. We could now put a check mark next to the category of "home" on Mom's Italy Checklist even though we had to remind ourselves of our good fortune each time we walked from our rented car to the entrance and stepped on snails, hearing crunch, crunch, crunch! No matter how many times I swept them to the grass, within hours the sidewalk was covered again. Nevertheless, excited that we now had room for real furniture I decided I wanted pieces that were bright, fun, and a bit crazy. I ordered a large yellow sofa, for which I waited excitedly, only to receive a cream-colored one. Undaunted, I ordered some yellow curtains instead.

More importantly, we filled this house with love, laughter, and fun. Every morning, I would wake up and switch on the music on our five-disc CD player. As the set list would evolve from classical to instrumental, Benjamin and Samuel would gear up for the finale of "rock out" time, often with the blaring tunes by Rush or a similar "Daddy's music" band. The boys would dance and run around, which was just what I wanted. If they didn't get that energy out of their systems early, the day would not go so smoothly.

We'd also play lots of board games, and with more time together we simply stumbled upon the kinds of silly, crazy rituals that can't help but make a family closer—sometimes literally. Our shower was very small, and for some reason I would end up with Bart and the boys joining me in there most mornings. Amid the laughter and the silliness—and, of course, careful parental monitoring of appropriate boundaries I would shout, "Why can't I just take a shower by myself anymore?" And we'd all laugh some more.

Every Tuesday, Bart and I would have date night, occasionally even hiring a sitter. Bart always kept his eye out for small ways to create romantic moments. I remember how we both had been admiring the top of a wall, probably thousands of years old, that we could see high above the autostrada, or freeway, as we drove to or from Avezzano. "It would be neat to go up there sometime. But how could you even find it?" I would say. One night Bart took me to dinner at a restaurant called L'Angolo D'Abruzzo. After dinner, he drove along the back roads and parked at the bottom of a small town. As we walked into the bar/coffee shop, every local turned to check out these two Americans. Bart spoke a few words to them in Italian and then guided me up through the town, over thousand-year-old foundations, until I found myself looking over the valley around us, with the autostrada below, realizing that we had arrived at the exact wall we had admired from the freeway. As we sat on this ancient wall, Bart said, "Do you know how extremely beautiful you are? And how much I love to kiss you?" I felt as if we were the only two people who existed in this world.

For date nights when we didn't go out, after the boys were in bed we'd play Scrabble, with Bart keeping a slight lead on me in the running score. Then out of the blue he would ask me to dance.

"Isn't it just like I told you it would be?" he asked me during one late-night dance. "I have you all to myself." I could now also put a check mark next to the category "Quality Couple Time."

The "Social and Leisure" category was practically off the charts, what with all the wonderful places we explored either as a family or with visiting friends. The Amalfi Coast was a consistent favorite. On one memorable excursion, we showed the area to my friend Martha and her husband Bob visiting from home. In the village of Amalfi, we all stayed in the Hotel Luna, a former monastery built in 1222, and as the boys slept we adults sat on the terrace dining on delicious local food we had gathered that day: meats, cheeses, bread, olives, and, of course, wine.

Bart and I were always happy to share these places with the boys, doing it our way. In Italy we quickly got used to having dinner at 8:00 pm or even later, and although you don't often see Italians eating out together as a family, we brought Benjamin and Samuel into the restaurants with us, and when they'd go to sleep at some point during the meal, as they inevitably would, I'd just push two chairs together and make a bed for them.

Of course, there were other categories on Mom's Italy Checklist that were a bit trickier, or even impossible, to check off. The "Cleanliness and Safety" category was always a tough one. On the winding drive along the Amalfi Coast or other similar places, you'd see busses, trucks, and semi trucks driving fast along roads narrower than some American driveways. It was not uncommon to have to back up to a wider section of road to let a tourist bus go by. A lot of times there were cliffs without guardrails on the sides of such roads so you looked down one hundred yards to crashing waves. And on any street of a city or town, you'd see dozens of kids with no helmets whipping around on scooters.

I learned from other Americans that it wasn't enough just to look out for cars when crossing a street or even walking along a sidewalk, if you were lucky to have one to walk along, especially on narrow streets. When you wanted to cross, you actually had to make eye contact with the person behind the wheel of an approaching vehicle and, hopefully, receive some sign that they knew you were there and wouldn't run you over. When we'd walk, I would hold Benjamin and Samuel's hands tightly. On our favorite walks to Bar 2000 to get the boys Popsicles, I would often see local Italians walking with their kids while shaking their fists at a driver and screaming, "You didn't stop!"

In Rome, it was not unusual to have to swerve around a car parked in the middle of a major thoroughfare while the driver ran into a café for coffee, which in Italy might take forty-five minutes or longer. "It's just a different culture," I would say, trying to explain these conditions to the boys. "It may be difficult for us to understand because we wouldn't do that, but that's just the way they are here. They're not rude or trying to do something bad to us."

I'd offer the same explanation in shops when no one would wait on us while Italians barged in front of us or when we would come upon an otherwise attractive park strewn with litter and debris. Once we observed a bus driver pull over on a main city street, open the front door, and stand at the top step while he relieved himself. That's the side of Italy most tourists do not see, or choose not to notice, but which those who live in the country long enough to call it home can't help but come upon every day.

In Italy, you simply get used to the beautiful and the ugly existing side by side. Even in a gorgeous spot like Positano, when you descend the five hundred steps to the beach, as you look out at the beautiful view you also have to navigate cigarette butts, assorted garbage, and the stench of urine from stray dogs and cats. You might approach a stunning church or fresco but have to sidestep merchants shoving dirty, smelly things in your face before you can get up close. Right outside The Church of St. Peter's Chains, one of our favorite spots in Rome, we'd stop by a food stand where Benjamin loved the fresh coconut. But as we walked away eating our treats, we'd be slapping our arms at all the napkins dancing in the breeze. Ah, but if you dared to be a woman with bare shoulders showing in a church you'd risk having a stranger rush up and put a shawl around you because it didn't "look right." The good-bad contrasts are illustrated in a lively and honest way in the memoir *Four Seasons in Rome* by Anthony Doerr, an American living in Italy with his wife and twin sons.

There were countless other unusual things to deal with that may not have been especially unclean or unsafe but that nevertheless challenged our ability to adjust. When I'd go shopping with the boys, I would have to deposit a coin to get a cart. In our first months there, I struggled to figure out which coin to put in, with something like 1,000 lire for every 50 cents. And then, just when I began to master that system of calculation, Italy switched to the euro. I always had a hard time figuring out which milk or water would taste "normal." And I had to keep a vigilant eye out for which magazines to block from the boys' view so I wouldn't have to answer the question "Why doesn't that girl have any clothes on, Mamma?"

Entering the bank was another challenge. It was a long process in which you had to pass through two doors. I had to send Benjamin first. While Samuel and I waited, he would go through one door, and, after it closed behind him, the door to the bank would open. Then I would send Samuel in next, and Benjamin would need to hold on to him for dear life until I could get through the doors since my whirlwind Samuel could destroy so much in a short period of time without guidance. Eventually we learned to accept or deal with all the challenges as best we could.

Bart had a different perspective on the culture from spending so much time at Micron with other Americans, and he could never get enough of the art, history, and architecture everywhere we visited. Of course, even Bart would sometimes lose his patience when driving directions led us astray or we faced some unexpected delay. "If you want to venture out and see places, you have to accept that these sorts of things will happen," I would gently chide him.

Samuel just loved to play and keep us on our toes wherever he was, and Benjamin pulled Italy close to his chest and hugged it with all his strength, appreciating the beauty around us everywhere we went in the country. For example, once, when we were outside the Colosseum in Rome, Benjamin pointed to a wall and said, "Mamma, you have to take a picture of me on that wall." It was off our route, we didn't really have time, but Benjamin persisted until we finally went with him to the exact spot he had in mind, posed him with vines coming down across his face, and took this special picture, aware of the beauty he had seen at that place. We later printed the picture to put in his bedroom.

There were also other times Benjamin showed his ability to keenly ob-serve the beauty around him and his wish to express it. Soon after we were settled in Italy, Bart and I had given Benjamin a sketch pad and told him anytime he saw something attractive that he wanted to capture, we would stop to let him draw it. He would often take us up on that offer. I remember him once wanting to spend time drawing a rock wall in Sienna, a town in the Tuscany area known for its medieval cityscape. Another time, in Florence, he pointed to an area behind some trees and said, "Mamma, look at the way the sun is coming through those trees. It's like heaven." He then guided me to the place and made a sketch, while I stood by in wonder.

Benjamin was curious about everything, and he could take almost anything in stride if you spent time explaining it to his satisfaction. When the tragedy of 9/11 happened just a few months into our time in Italy, Benjamin asked me why it had happened—a parental challenge.

"Well, Benjamin, there are people who fight against each other because they have different beliefs or faiths. Unfortunately, instead of listening to each other, they decide to hurt each other."

Benjamin flashed his deep-thinking look and replied, "Maybe they just need to understand each other's language. If they understood each other's language, then they would understand each other and they wouldn't have to fight." This insight made him even more determined to learn the "other language" of Italian.

Some people teased Benjamin for being too dramatic or judged him for being too deep. But I knew that was just who he was. He took after his mother. I used to get teased for being too deep when I was growing up, but over time, and through many experiences, I came to accept that if I didn't think deeply perhaps I would not have survived this tragedy.

Bart and I signed up for Italian language classes in June and stuck with it through our stay. I have a vivid memory of one of our last lessons. I had to miss the previous class, and when we began, our instructor, Cristina, said, "Last time I asked Bart to explain what you meant to him in Italian. Now I want you to do the same. Tell me in Italian what Bart means to you." That was easy; I said, *"La luce della mia vita"* ("The light of my life"). Learning the rest of the language was not so easy, and from the start Benjamin pulled well ahead of us. When we'd go to the store and I would at least use my *grazie, scusi, per favore,* Benjamin would say, "Mom, you're speaking Italian. Good Job!" His interactions with Italian kids and teachers at day care helped him speak the language more often and more naturally.

Benjamin's obvious learning ability required that we made sure he had access to good schooling in Italy. As a rising first grader, Benjamin was facing an important transition. We wanted to find the best possible way to keep him learning. At first we went along with a suggestion from the Micron folks to use a private teacher they had arranged for him. But when we discovered Benjamin was to be the only student, I knew that wasn't going to be in his best interests. "I'm not concerned about Benjamin academically, but I am concerned about him socially," I said to Bart. "He needs a classroom environment." But where could we find a school that would meet his needs? we wondered.

We began looking at a Catholic school connected to a convent and orphanage in Avezzano. The teachers there were the *suore*, or sisters, one of whom, Sister Carla, spoke English fluently. I was eager to meet her, and being used to scouting schools and teachers in Idaho, I came to prepared with questions: What are your teaching methods? Can you show me a sample lesson plan? As I soon learned, she did not have answers to my questions. Such questions had never been asked of her by other parents, who assumed that the only way of teaching was directly from schoolbooks. Perhaps that was when I realized the cultural differences, even in elementary school, would be an educational process for both Benjamin and his mom.

But that did not worry me because from the moment I met Sister Carla I felt an indescribable connection to her. Our interactions made me recall how I wanted to be a nun when I was a girl in Weiser, Idaho. More than that, simply being around her gave me an indefinable sense of peace and made me to want to get to know her better. Little did I realize just how well I would get to know this very different sister.

Benjamin also hit it off with Sister Carla from the start, though he wasn't quite as comfortable with the school itself initially. While we observed the school in action on Class Day, we noticed that the kids were acting unruly during an organized activity. As Benjamin watched Sister Carla playing her guitar and Mother Superior trying to talk above the noise, he was unusually clingy and had tears in his eyes, reactions very different from his usual behavior.

"Why won't they just be quiet for the teacher's song?" he asked. "The kids are so rude."

"Oh, I don't think they're rude," I responded. "They're just excited about the opening of school. I'm sure it will get quieter once they are in their classrooms."

Even though I was not totally convinced of my prediction, I wanted Benjamin to think positively about the school atmosphere, and within days he loved it there. We enrolled Samuel for preschool at the same school, but unfortunately his assigned teacher, Sister Pasquina, didn't speak English or play the guitar, although she tried her best to make Samuel feel welcome. "*Ti voglio bene!*" she would loudly proclaim as she pinched Samuel's cheeks. I would have to remind him again and again that the words meant "I love you" because, when exposed to her gruff manner, Samuel didn't exactly buy it. I decided that Samuel would only attend for two short days a week, just enough to give me some peace at home and him some social time. Before long Samuel was telling Sister Carla he wanted to be in her classroom. When she asked him why, he said, "Because of all the beautiful girls" as he moved his eyebrows up and down, making her laugh. By then, we felt confident enough about the educational possibilities at the school to be able to put a check mark next to "School" on Mom's Italy Checklist.

Of all the other items on her list, one stood out, waiting to be checked off: "Mom's First Visit." While I did appreciate the rare opportunity to have some distance from our relatives back home so I could have more uninterrupted time and energy for my family, I still missed Mom terribly. During those first few months, we talked frequently on the phone. I also wrote her an email every morning so she would have all the latest news, and she did the same for me. I might tell her about a dinner I hosted for friends, sharing the details of serving artichoke dip, sloppy chicken and peppered ribs with baked potatoes, carrots and onions, and apple pie for dessert. She'd write back: "I'm trying to be skinny before my trip to Italy, but I have to admit I just had a dinner of three chicken enchiladas with sour cream and beans, a king-sized margarita, chips, and salsa. At least I ordered shredded lettuce with my meal to make me feel it was a salad." Mom ate anything and was no bigger than a toothpick—I wished I had those genes.

Now I would finally get to see Mom. Mom was to fly to Italy on September 15 with Aunt Doris and stay for an entire month. Then, in November, Dad was planning to come to stay for two full months, including spending Christmas with us in Austria. I still had that ominous inner feeling about him that I experienced the day before we left Boise, but I could only hope everything would be fine. I believed that having a unique experience of living in a foreign country would never be complete until I was able to share it with others I loved. Finally, that was going to happen. Everything about the Kraft Family Italian Adventure was coming together—or so I thought.

Chapter 6
The Emergency Phone Call

FOUR DAYS BEFORE MOM WAS TO FLY TO ROME, the horror of 9/11 occurred. As Americans, we huddled closer to one another in our Micron community in Avezzano, but we soon felt the love and support of the Italian people all around us. An entry in my journal at the time read:

Dear Lord,

There is no way to explain this tragedy, and I know you are crying alongside of us. There is a feeling of sadness, disbelief, and anger paralyzing our lives. People across the world have been affected by this cruel act.

As Americans, we need to allow others to grieve alongside of us. Help us open our hearts and gain strength from numbers, not from anger. We are a strong nation and will become stronger not by fighting hate with hate but by pulling together and taking action against those involved. Give us clarity and guide us in the direction you want us to go. Help America distinguish between the evildoers and the innocent, no matter their race, color, or religion. Let us take this tragic event and stand tall, for we all are your children, and with your help the world can unite against such evil. Amen.

Because regular commercial flights did not immediately resume out of the United States after the attacks, we weren't sure what would happen to Mom's plan to fly out of Detroit with Aunt Doris. Jody and Sue were nervous about Mom getting on a plane at all, reminding me that she had never been out of the country except to Victoria, Canada. This was one time I actually was *not* nervous. In those first days after 9/11, I believed that she would be safer in Italy with us than in the United States.

Eventually, Mom got on a flight from Boise to Minneapolis, although even domestic flights had yet to resume anything close to a regular schedule. The next leg of the journey was proving more difficult. At the airport, Mom wound up sitting next to the pilot assigned to the delayed flight, and when she told him about trying to get to Rome to visit us, he vowed, "I'll get you to your daughter. I just need a plane."

Finally a plane did arrive, and Mom was overjoyed to find Aunt Doris waiting for her at the gate. That plane bound for Italy was, as far as I knew, the first commercial flight out of the country after the attacks.

In Avezzano, Mom's grandsons were getting ready for her arrival. Samuel's fourth birthday was September 12, and we made sure to arrange for a lively and fun celebration despite the tragedy that had just occurred. Benjamin liked to dress in the favorite color of anyone visiting with us, so, knowing that Grandma liked yellow, he wore yellow boots as part of his outfit for going to the airport, complete with a tie and even some of Bart's cologne. Mom had gone all out for him, too. She had purchased a dress suit in robin's egg blue, Benjamin's favorite color at the time. Samuel couldn't wait for a big hug from Grandma, though he stayed glued to me at the airport so he wouldn't be overwhelmed by the activity.

I was determined to give Mom a taste of Italy right away, so on the way back to Avezzano from Rome we stopped in Tivoli, where we visited the Villa d'Este, the estate where a French king had diverted the river through his land with enormous fountains. We had lunch at Castel Madama, where Mom and Aunt Doris were startled to see how people parked and drove on the sidewalk. When we bought some gorgeous long-stem lilies, Mom asked, "Is this a special place for buying flowers like that?" When I told her that flower bouquets costing $100 or more back home were available cheaply everywhere in Italy, she was amazed.

When we got to our home, we moved Mom's things into Benjamin's room, since he slept with Samuel in Samuel's room, and we gave Aunt Doris the playroom on the third floor. Benjamin and Samuel had been busy decorating both of their rooms, complete with pictures on the walls, flowers, candles, and pillows neatly arranged.

"Make sure you don't pull the rope or you'll make the alarm go off," Benjamin told Grandma.

Since the next day was a Sunday, we got up early for an excursion to Sorrento. After some fun sightseeing, Mom smiled as she gazed at the same view I had described to her on the phone while sipping cognac with Bart soon after our arrival in Italy.

As usual, Mom took charge organizing things right away. "I'll help you make this place feel even more homey," she told me as she looked around our house. For several days, we ventured to stores to buy new odds and ends and then brainstormed about what changes to make in my home decor. Because we had only been in the house a few weeks, I still had many unpacked boxes, and as Mom and I slowly worked through them it felt like being in our new house in Eagle with her again. She also helped me better coordinate my shopping and food preparation. Mom the project manager was back on the job.

Mom also resumed her role of being my supporter, a voice of reassurance to combat my insecurities. When I told her I was anxious about my weight, she said, "But you look so beautiful!" When I admitted that I sometimes felt intimidated at the idea of going out in the Avezzano community because no one spoke English, she said, "But you're so brave. A lot of people would never put themselves in the position of living here in the first place." When I whined about having to run up the hill to turn the power back on during the frequent outages in our house with everyone watching me, she said, "Well, when it happens the next time we'll all put on our bathrobes and really give them a show. We'll be the talk of all of Italy!"

Yes, Mom was still my anchor. She was a woman who enjoyed giving advice but also being right. Although Mom was nine years younger than her sibling Aunt Doris, Mom often approached her sister as an equal, or even her superior. While on a shopping trip in Rome, Mom bought a leather jacket with a fur collar. Aunt Doris liked it, too, but hesitated buying one, saying, "But what if I find something better in another store before we go home?"

"I can't believe you're not buying this right now," Mom replied with a shrug. Sure enough, just before they were to fly out of Rome Aunt Doris returned to that store and bought the same leather coat, much to Mom's satisfaction.

On another outing, the three of us headed to the small town of Albe, about half an hour from home, to have lunch at a restaurant Bart and I had discovered, with a gorgeous panoramic view of the valley below. Getting there meant driving up a narrow dirt road, and when I spotted a car coming down, I determined that I would need to back up and pull over at the next open area. The trouble was I was not so good at backing up. We wound up in the ditch, surrounded by Italians telling us exactly what to do to get the car out so other cars could get by. Somehow they were sure that Mom, only a size six, should sit on the hood of the car to give it weight while they tried to push it out. She went along with it for a while but then laughingly explained, "It's too hot. I can't sit on that anymore!" The Italians, not understanding English, kept having her get back on the car hood, and she kept jumping off until I finally remembered the Italian word for hot: *Caldo!* We at last liberated our car, only to find a huge dent and scratch from a tree.

When the Boise folks back at the Micron plant heard this story, their wheels started to spin. They loved coming up with their own names for Italian restaurants they would frequent: they called one place The White House and another the A-Frama because it resembled one of their favorite bars in Boise named A-Frame. They soon decided that henceforth the restaurant in Albe would be known as Car Crash.

When we took Mom and Aunt Doris to Pompeii, the ancient town that had been buried in ashes when Mt. Vesuvius erupted, Mom was so intrigued that she bought a video about the history of the place to watch together later. I don't remember much about that video, but I vividly recall, and still like to play, the home video we shot during one of our typical morning rock-outs with the boys. Mom was still getting ready upstairs when the music started blaring and the video camera was turned on, but you can clearly see her grand entrance and the carefree manner in which she began to dance. That was my mom: ever willing to have some fun, no matter how silly she might look to others.

Mom and Aunt Doris both helped with housework, especially the laborious one-hour laundry routine, during which it was not possible to run any other household appliances. Aunt Doris proclaimed Mom "The Laundry Queen." Mom also enjoyed taking the boys to school and joining in their fun and games at home, and she was gracious enough to look after them a few times so Bart and I could go out.

For those four wonderful weeks, Mom and I didn't talk together much differently than we would on the phone or through email. We just shared that special communication that occurs when you don't need to talk at all, when you're just together and you know the secrets of your bond, one never to be broken.

Far too soon it was time for a last whirlwind tour of the scenes in Rome before Mom and Aunt Doris would leave. Aunt Doris appeared especially impressed with the history, explaining to me all about how St. Peter was buried in AD 64 and everything else about St. Peter's Basilica. I felt proud to be able to show them something so magnificent. Of course, we wanted them to see the Sistine Chapel, but after enduring the hour-plus wait in cramped quarters with hundreds of tourists we looked up at the ceiling to appreciate the famous frescos and concluded, "For all that, it might not be as magnificent as the Vatican."

After spending the last night at the Hilton in Rome, as we tearfully parted Mom was ready with another one of her reassuring reminders. "You know I'll be back as soon as I can," she said, "maybe in March."

A few weeks after Mom left, Dad's visit was approaching. I had never shaken free of the sense I had in Boise that I would never see him again, but I sure wanted to. Spending two months with my father in Italy would be so special. We had always been close; in many ways, he still considered me his little girl. And he relished every chance to play with his grandsons. Like Bart, Dad also would have a real appreciation for the history and architecture of Italy. I would have so much to show him!

A week before Dad was to fly out, I told Bart that something changed for me. "Dad is really going to come. I must have been wrong before with those scary thoughts. I *am* going to see him again! It's going to happen," I announced.

"I told you," Bart said with a big grin.

I went to bed that night feeling peaceful and happy, but when the phone rang at 6:00 am I instantly knew why.

"What's wrong with Dad?" were the first words I spoke to Jody.

"Dad had a stroke. We're not sure he's going to make it," Jody said.

With Bart's help, we got the rest of the story. Dad had been in his garage looking for a particular suitcase to pack for Italy. He had had to climb up a ladder to reach it, then had a stroke and fell. He had had enough sense to call for help, but in his confusion he didn't dial 911 but 991. Luckily, he had had plans with a friend that day, and the friend, knowing my dad to never be late, called the police. They found Dad in his chair, four hours after the accident, barely alive.

Bart and I and the boys got on the first flight back home. On the plane, not knowing whether Dad would still be alive when we got there, my feelings from before we had left Boise about never seeing him again washed over me. I also remembered another one of my moments of "inner knowing," which had proven to be correct. In September, while driving home from a trip to Orvieto with Mom and Aunt Doris, we were trying to arrive home for the boys' bedtime. I looked at the clock and whispered so no one in the backseat could hear, "Look at the clock. We just bombed Afghanistan." After I put the boys to bed at home, we turned on the news to learn that at the very moment I had said this, the United States had indeed begun bombing Afghanistan in response to 9/11.

Reflecting on my premonitions during the flight to Boise made for an anxious journey. When we finally arrived, Dad was alive, but he looked very frail, hardly resembling the dad I knew. The stroke had caused extensive damage, and he needed major surgery to remove a blood clot from his brain. So my premonition about not seeing him again seemed to have manifested in one sense. Apparently, my premonition had meant that I wouldn't see him as I had known him, that the next time I would be in his presence he would be changed. From the moment I got there, I took turns with my siblings visiting Dad so he would have someone close to him at all times. It was clear that after a long period of hospitalization we would need to find a nursing home for him, but our hopes were that he would become lucid enough for an assisted living facility. One thing I did know was that I would not be going back to Avezzano anytime soon.

Bart stayed a week before he had to get back to his job in Italy. We decided that I would remain in Boise with Benjamin and Samuel, and Bart would come back for a few days over Christmas. We couldn't see beyond that.

As we drove Bart to the airport, even Bart remembered my words the day before we had left for Italy: "I will never see Dad again." Bart also brought up that moment in Italy when I had tuned in to the start of the bombing in Afghanistan without having seen or heard anything about it.

"So many of your predictions are coming true, it's starting to weird me out," he said.

"I know," I replied. "Me, too."

As we hugged and kissed, he looked into my eyes with a quizzical gaze. "So, do you think I should get on the plane?" he asked with his silly grin.

"Of course!" I said. "I love you tons."

As I rode down the escalator, lovingly watching Bart walk through security, I heard these words buzzing around in my head: *It isn't yet, Jill, but you won't grow old with him.* "Jill, stop thinking such morbid thoughts!" I muttered aloud.

The next days and weeks in Boise were a blur. For a couple of weeks I put Benjamin in the school where Jody taught so he wouldn't fall far behind in first grade, and I also found suitable day care for Samuel, so I could devote most of my time and energy to watching over Dad. It was strange communicating with Bart via email, but I was pleased to hear that in his off hours he still managed to see more of the cultural places that fed his soul. One visit was to the National Archaeological Museum of Naples, where Bart was fascinated by the mummies and sculptures of Roman emperors and Greek mythological figures. It was somehow important to me that the Kraft Family Italian Adventure was continuing in some form.

Still, as the time approached for Bart to come to Boise for Christmas, I was very excited to see him. The day I was to pick him up I changed outfits four times before driving to the airport while the boys were at Grandma's. When Bart walked through the doors, my eyes filled with tears and my body quivered. I was again looking at the most handsome man I had ever known. When he looked admiringly at me from a distance, I felt like we were meeting for our first date.

Christmas was sad without Dad, but at least the rest of us were together again as a family. There were many moments when we were able to laugh, and many when we had to cry. Mainly our whole family supported and loved one another, making us feel stronger than we had for quite a while.

"Well, this is the worst thing I imagine can happen to us, and we're making it," my sister Sue remarked, to which I had a sudden response I could not hold back: "I *pray* this is the worst thing that can happen to us."

Chapter 7
Teaching the Children of Sacro Coure

WATCHING MY DAD STRUGGLE to recover from the severe effects of his stroke was difficult during those long winter weeks in Idaho. Leaving him in Boise to return to Italy on January 6 was excruciating. I wanted to monitor the care he was receiving, to comfort him. Instead, I was thousands of miles away with my own family, who also needed me. At times I felt I was leaving everything on my sister Jody's shoulders; but Mom also stepped up, propelled by the caring and compassion she maintained for her ex-husband. Through emails and phone calls, I kept abreast of the latest news. Occasionally, I even talked to my dad, and I was greatly encouraged by hearing him sound more alert within two weeks after I left.

But I wanted to be doing more. Helping others was a part of my nature, going back to volunteering in the Big Brothers/Big Sisters Program when I was young. I also had volunteered for Make-a-Wish Foundation, where I served as the main coordinator for their silent auction and assisted in organizing other fundraising events. So I decided that as long as I was going to be living in Italy for several more months, and I couldn't be at home to help Dad, I was going to find some way to offer my time and energy to a worthy cause in Italy. The only question was where.

Our growing connection to Instituto Sacro Coure—the Institute of Sacred Heart—the school Benjamin and Samuel had been attending in Avezzano, prompted me to consider volunteering there in some capacity. Founded in 1894, it was more than a school. It included a convent where the sisters lived, and an orphanage that functioned as a foster home for up to twenty-five children, ages three through adolescence. Many kids stayed for extended periods of time while one or both parents struggled with serious life issues. Some kids remained at Sacro Coure until they were sent off to live independently at age eighteen. When Benjamin and Samuel went back to school there in January, we were all feeling more connected to the institution. Samuel, who in September had struggled to fit into such a different environment where everyone spoke Italian, was now more willing to join the other four-year-olds for play. He also was growing more excited about learning, including mastering the ability to write the *A* and the *M* in his name all by himself, prompted by me telling him the *M* looked like mountains and Benjamin telling him that running a finger over each eyebrow made an *M* on the face.

Benjamin, meanwhile, was speaking Italian for half an hour at a time. He also began taking the guitar we had bought for him to school because Sister Carla volunteered to teach him how to play it if he finished his lessons early each day. "I'm going to be in a band and be a rock star, Mamma," he vowed. Every day, after he got his work done, either Sister Carla would teach him a new chord on the guitar or he could continue working on his weekly art project. He was the only one in his class who got to do this, most likely as an incentive for him to finish his work because he got bored easily. This was a boy whose mind never rested, like when he taught himself multiplication one afternoon at home. For his art projects, he could use anything in the room and make whatever he wanted. Usually the projects were made for people he loved. I had never received one until he gave me a poem: "Love, love, love, that love is the love in sid you!" I knew he meant "inside," but I would always cherish it just the way he had written it. It was the last poem he ever wrote.

To explore the possibility of volunteering at Sacro Coure, I began learning more about how it functioned. Curious to know what circumstances led to the children winding up in the Sacro Coure orphanage, I asked Sister Carla. The stories she told me about these children's parents deeply saddened me and enhanced my appreciation for the service the orphanage was providing for them.

Yet I imagined that those children felt as if they were living in a school where up to six kids slept in one bedroom and had one classroom with standard desks and a TV, along with a barren recreation room. In such a highly structured environment, they had very little opportunity for any kind of individual creative expression. Day after day they were told what to do and how to behave, and then many, with few everyday skills, would be thrust at age eighteen into a country rampant with unemployment. I decided to offer these kids an opportunity to experience a new way of learning that entailed opportunities for creative expression, just as Sister Carla was enhancing Benjamin's opportunities for creative expression. Maybe through simple art projects and other creative endeavors I could help open new doors for some of them, I thought.

Benjamin and Samuel were totally on board with the idea, which was not surprising since my boys loved all kinds of creative expression. The one Italian TV show I allowed them to watch was *Art Attack*, a Disney-like program in which the host would finish an art project in thirty minutes. One day soon after we got back from Boise, Benjamin moved our furniture around to form a gigantic heart that was only visible from above. "You see, Mom," he explained, "you can make art out of anything."

It took a little convincing to get permission from the nun in charge of the orphanage to teach there, but with Sister Carla's help I was soon cleared to teach a weekly afternoon art class. I launched my creative arts class the first week in February. The turnout was small: just three girls. "The boys are too wild," I was told when I asked why they were kept off to the side doing homework instead of joining in reading a book about coral reefs then making ocean creatures out of the colored salt dough I had brought in. The girls didn't quite grasp the idea of molding something related to the ocean, but they had a great time anyway. They also didn't understand that they were to leave their sea creatures out for the clay to harden. When they quickly shoved all the clay on the table into a bag, Benjamin's eyes got misty seeing his beautiful crab destroyed. But it was a start, and I must have passed the test because the next time thirteen children, including boys, turned up for my class.

During the second class, we made erupting volcanoes. I had the kids put pink salt dough with chocolate sprinkles on the outside of a bottle containing vinegar. Then we added baking soda and watched it erupt. The children loved it! One nun even took pictures, and while another appeared not to be used to the kind of mess we were making, I could tell from their whispering and laughing that they admired what this crazy American woman was seeking to do. I went on to guide the children in making candy volcanoes. I gave each of them a plastic plate and had them wad up some tinfoil and cover it with brown frosting. Then they wrapped string black licorice around it and put pink bubble gum on for the lava. To complete the scene, I gave them Smarties for flowers and crunched hard candies for the grass. As I watched the children's faces, I sensed they were enjoying the experience of artistic expression.

Buoyed by my success, and assisted by a girl from the orphanage who spoke enough English to translate my instructions to the others, I next invited them to use clay to create an expression of what they wanted to be when they grew up, or what their greatest gift from God was. I smiled when I noticed that the gift Benjamin depicted was to sing. While it was a bit frustrating not to be able to ask all the Italian children what they were shaping, I could tell they were taking it very seriously. I told them that next week they could paint their clay creations, but after that project I was directed to leave the paint at home. The sisters had limits regarding how much of a mess we could make!

One Tuesday in March when Easter was approaching, I had the children make crosses out of colored tissue. Between classes, I kept imagining more creative endeavors that would lift the spirits of the children while continuing to win over the nuns. Though the sisters were very devoted to keeping these children healthy, there was no doubt in my mind that they could also benefit from becoming a bit more creative.

Not only had I found a way to give my time and energy to a worthy cause, but my work at the orphanage also had an added benefit: to educate my own children about the importance and joy of helping others. From watching me prepare and lead my classes, Benjamin understood how volunteering to help others makes you feel good. He asked me how I used to assist at Make-a-Wish Foundation in Boise and took such activity to heart. Now his thoughtful side had been stirred. One day he came to me to announce his own carefully conceived plan to help others. "We're going to have an American party," he began. "We'll invite all our friends here and feed them American food like hot dogs and hamburgers. Then we'll put on music and dance. Everyone who comes will pay ten dollars for a ticket, and all the money will go to the poor and needy here in Italy," he said. My eyes were already moist with pride, but Benjamin made it clear there was more to his vision. "Then, when we move back to Boise we'll have an Italian party," he explained. "We'll serve all Italian food. The money for those tickets will be for the poor and needy in Boise. You see, Mom, wherever we go, we can help those in need."

How on earth can a first grader come up with such an inspiring idea? I wondered then. Why would someone with such a beautiful heart be gone in one month? I wonder now.

While Benjamin's vision melted my heart, the logistics created a challenge. Back home, if you raised money you could just donate it to the Salvation Army and they would buy food and clothing to distribute to those in need, but in Italy the process wasn't so simple. Sister Carla suggested a short-term solution. Sacro Coure had scheduled a fund-raising event for poor children in Africa, and she thought Benjamin would enjoy getting dressed up and selling tickets at the door. "Perfect," I said. Benjamin didn't need any coaxing and looked forward to the big event in April.

At that point my volunteer work at the orphanage and many of my other routine activities would have to wait because Mom was coming back for a second visit, from March 16 to 30, which we had timed for spring break at school in Boise so Jody and Sarah could come, too. We would have two weeks to share with family, including my special niece Sarah, the cousin the boys loved so dearly, two weeks to show those close to my heart the country I was beginning to love more each day. Although I still struggled with the negatives—trash everywhere, prostitutes along the roads between towns, the stench of urine in alleys, the jostling crowds in cafés, the Italians who would shove you out of line at stores just because they didn't care for Americans—I had come to understand that every place has positives and negatives, and the positives here were certainly abundant.

My goal was to look every Italian I would meet in the eye and say *"Buon giorno"* without judgment.

While we continued to enjoy the beauty, the architecture, and the history, there was also something else I began to appreciate about Italy. While in the States for several weeks after Dad's stroke, I had been struck by the contrast between the size of things in Italy and in the United States. Our homes in the United States tend to be so much bigger than homes in Italy. Portions of the food in restaurants or the cappuccinos served in our favorite coffee shops are huge compared with those in Italy, and we waste so much of it. In Italian restaurants and cafés, the portions are smaller. And yet the Italian people seem to appreciate whatever they have, no matter how small, rather than constantly striving for more and bigger things. This lesson would stick with me.

We took advantage of opportunities for exploration and adventure, and usually learned something about Italian culture in the process. One unseasonably warm sixty-degree February afternoon we went to a sandy beach between Naples and Rome. It was a beautiful spot, with big cactus and palm trees. The boys burned up so much energy playing in the sand they soon took off their jackets and sweaters and darted along the edge of the water in shirtsleeves. When the locals on the beach, still dressed in their heavy winter coats, were aghast, we learned that Italians dress for the time of year not the actual weather of the day. We also discovered the intriguing town of Gaeta; here the boys got to explore the grotto where, in AD 846, pirates would hide during the day before coming out to invade the town at night.

Fortunately, in many large historical places I was able to let the boys run ahead of us, a welcome freedom for two children trained to listen for their mom to yell, "Freeze!" then instantly become statues of what they wanted to be: a motorcycle or truck for Samuel, an opera singer, flamingo, or dolphin for Benjamin.

We also began to mix more with the Italian people at events and restaurants, making us feel still more at home. One night we attended a soccer match at Olympic Stadium in Rome. Bart joked that since the home team

Roma's rivalry with the opponent, Perugia, was not so intense, riots would probably not be a threat. But when someone from Perugia threw fireworks from the stands onto the field, I began to wonder. Ultimately, Rome won 1-0, and we enjoyed the postgame planned fireworks with the rest of the crowd.

We also discovered that in some restaurants in Italy, if you show an interest in their wine cellar they'll invite you down for a look and perhaps some stories about the wine. We were becoming more and more attuned to great wines and found that Italians not only love to drink wine they also love to tell stories about wine, such as the following story we heard in Orvieto when we were showing Mom and Aunt Doris around. Back in the year AD 1100, Bishop Fugger was traveling from Germany to Rome for the coronation of King Henry V. He sent his quartermaster ahead to scout the inns on his route and the quality of wine they served. If the quartermaster liked an inn, he wrote on the wall: "*Est*," which means "This is it" in Latin. He liked the wine at one inn in the town of Montefiascone so much that he wrote: "*Est! Est!! Est!!!*" Apparently the bishop agreed with this rating because he skipped the coronation and never left the town. Every year on the anniversary of his death, the locals pour a flask of this brand of wine on his grave.

We also learned more about Italian traditions from Bart's Italian co-worker Emilio and his wife Antonella, who had become close friends. When I taught Antonella how to make pancakes from a mix I had brought from Boise, she liked them so much we made them for dinner at midnight the night of the soccer match. In return, she taught me how to make pasta from scratch. Knowing that Sheri, my friend from Boise, had taken a course on how to make authentic gnocchi, a potato pasta, I then invited her over one day so we could exchange our Italian cooking skills. I wore out my arms from the hours of rolling all that pasta, but I felt grateful to be having these experiences.

As a family, we didn't even have to leave our neighborhood in Avezzano to feel invigorated with the wonders of being in Italy. We felt a part of our surroundings as we enjoyed the steady stream of stray dogs and cats in the area, including a German shepherd pup. While Benjamin named the dog Sneakers because he was so good at sneaking around, the name that stuck was Samuel's "Crane Digger" because it made us laugh. And we took advantage of our family time together to watch many movies. When Benjamin saw *Beauty and the Beast* for the first time, he said to me, "I will be the beast, and you will be the beauty." We all laughed through family games of Clue, and often after the boys had gone to sleep Bart and I would get down to serious competition playing Scrabble. I was staying neck-and-neck with this former high school valedictorian in Scrabble games. In mid-March, the score was Bart 422, Jill 414, and he had only passed me by earning 128 points for the word *squeeze*! Aware of the necessity of maintaining peace in the family despite the competition, one day I even emailed Mom: "I have won two games in a row so I had to let Bart win one!"

The boys loved to put on skits and had a good one ready for Bart's birthday, on March 12. They made tissue hats and had a special way of presenting them to Sheri and I. Benjamin started things off with a grand introduction of himself, saying, "Now presenting Benjamin Joel Kraft!" The highlight was when Benjamin presented "Samuel Garfield Kraft." Samuel came out grooving to his own beat, stopped midway, and, while moving his eyebrows up and down, said, "Sheri, you need to go look in a mirror, because you are a beautiful girl!" *Beautiful* had become one of his favorite words, and he said it with that Italian male flair.

Benjamin also enjoyed talking like an Italian. Our Italian friends told us he did not even have an accent. One day, while going out to the Sora market with Emilio and Antonella, Benjamin rode in their car with them. As we arrived, Emilio and Antonella got out of their car laughing hysterically, but Benjamin was serious. Apparently, he had said, "*Io sono fame*" ("I am hungry")! Antonella had replied, "No, *Io ho fame*" ("I have hunger"). Benjamin had corrected her, repeating how he said it first, and then she had repeated the Italian way to say it. Becoming frustrated, Benjamin had said, "*Tu non sie niente nella Italiano*" ("You know nothing in Italian"). As sweet as Benjamin was, he was strong in his convictions.

We had never been closer as a family, and Bart had never been more relaxed. He was making good on his vow to claim time for us, and he was having a good time himself. Bart had always had a hearty laugh, but even his boss Wayne noted that he seemed to laugh more often and more freely in Italy than he had back in Boise. One evening he turned to me and said, "I would stay home all day if I could, just to watch Samuel!" Bart loved the Italian people and the acceptance he felt from them. He never tired of the magnificent art and architecture, and he was always on the lookout for some new activity to try. When spring came, he was going to head out into the forest on a truffle-hunting expedition, where dogs search for those unusual yet delicious mushrooms.

As Bart and I grew ever closer, I sensed that he felt proud of me for creating a warmth and joy that could be felt upon entering a truly happy home in this place so far from everything we had known. Of course, we were doing it together, but perhaps Bart was seeing a different side of me that made him feel I was as intelligent and capable as he was.

Amid so much tranquility and family harmony, I still had moments of anxiety about my premonition concerning the family. One evening I had become especially concerned while reading a story to Benjamin and Samuel and noticing that Samuel had an unusually serious look.

"I'm going to go live with Jesus," he said.

"Yes, Samuel," I replied softly, "we all will someday."

"No, Mamma, I will go live with Jesus *soon,*" he said.

"Samuel, you can't talk that way," I said, trying to keep my voice calm. "We all will, but for now we need to live long, healthy lives to honor him."

Then I watched as Benjamin leaned over and put his arms around me. "Don't worry, Mamma," he said, "you'll be okay." I let the moment pass because the boys shifted their attention, but it didn't fade so quickly inside me. As soon as I heard Bart arrive home, I ran out the door into his arms. I explained what had just happened and the fear welling within me.

"I promise, Jill, that won't happen," he said.

"But you can't promise," I argued, crying. Bart's hug finally soothed my anxiety enough that by the next morning I was focused on Mom, Jody, and Sarah's coming visit.

The boys had been ready for weeks. From the day we got back to Italy in January, Samuel could hardly stop thinking of Grandma. He would go around the house saying, "She is so *beautiful*, and I miss her so much!" He thought we ought to be able to get on a plane and visit her every day. Benjamin was eager to show "Sarrrah" his school, explaining that "while in Italy, I can only call her Sarrrah because that is her name here." He assured me that he would make it a point to translate some of the Italian words the children were speaking to her so she wouldn't feel out of place.

I had been busy putting together our sightseeing itinerary. Since Bart had been given extra time off, we had more options. Mom already had seen most of our favorite places in central and southern Italy, so I decided that we would head north to Venice, Florence, and other exciting new terrain. With Venice eight hours away, that would mean lots of driving, but we had grown accustomed to driving in Italy, with its narrow, winding roads and drivers who sometimes made you feel like you were playing bumper cars. While Bart was alone in Italy during the time I was in Boise with Dad, he had written a hilarious poem he titled "Drive Like an Italian," to be sung to the tune of the Bangles' song "Walk Like an Egyptian." I had backed into a ditch. Among the Micron contingent, Jonathan had wrecked his car on his way to work one day, though he had fortunately not been injured, and Brian had totaled his car in an accident in which he also was not hurt.

We all understood that seeing everything Italy had to offer meant dealing with the crazy driving in the country. For nine months, we dealt with it so we were not going to let it be a roadblock for this long-anticipated family trip. I was doing everything I could to make sure this would be a visit none of us would ever forget.

Chapter 8
The Accident

AFTER MOM, JODY, AND SARAH ARRIVED, we all looked forward to sightseeing together with great anticipation. Then, while we were preparing to depart, Sarah and the boys decided they would put on an Easter show for Mom, Jody, and me. They were thrilled to be together performing once again. The stage was outside on our lawn. After handing Benjamin and Sarah our tickets, Jody and I were politely escorted to our straight, uncomfortable chairs, while Mom was ceremoniously led to a relaxing-looking lawn chair. As Jody and I observed, *look how we rate!* Mom very dramatically got into her chair, which immediately collapsed. Seeing that Mom was fine, Jody and I howled as we watched her scramble to get back up and make the adjustments to the chair that the kids hadn't quite mastered. Soon Benjamin hushed us, reminding us that they were enacting a serious story of Jesus on the cross.

Benjamin, in the role of Jesus, put his usual deep feeling into his character, raising his arms above his head and moaning to show his pain. Sarah narrated what we were seeing at such great length that Benjamin, holding his arms up in the cross formation, kept shaking his hands in hopes of her soon finishing. They were doing a wonderful job, and we gave them our full attention...until Samuel became the kind of distraction we had all come to adore. Because he couldn't sit still, as always, he grabbed a bucket and put it over his head then somehow got a twenty-foot chain wrapped around himself and started spinning in his best attempt to break free from this "monster." After first making sure he was in no danger of hurting himself and that he wasn't getting frustrated, I focused again on enjoying the show. But Benjamin and Sarah, who had also turned to watch Samuel, seemed more concerned than we were, not because they thought Samuel might strangle himself but because they were worried he might mess up his big moment in their production. "Samuel, Samuel!" Sarah finally blurted out. "It's time for your part!"

After Sarah did her best to unwind Samuel from the chain, he looked our way and proclaimed, "The end." I couldn't tell if we were clapping more than laughing or vice versa, but we gave the show our highest reviews. The family visit was in full swing!

We then proceeded to show our guests around our favorite local spots. Sarah visited Sacro Coure with Benjamin, who introduced her to everyone and made sure she felt welcome. She even agreed to wear a school uniform. I showed Mom and Jody the market in Sora and stopped in the town of Caserta, known for its beautiful ceramics. Toward the end of that first week, Bart was free to join us for several days, so we packed up our Renault Espace minivan for our excursion north.

We spent Friday night at Villa Gaidello, outside of Bologna, an *agriturismo* (bed and breakfast) that served a seven-course meal. It was a beautiful spot with a pond with swans and a wide-open area where Sarah, Benjamin, and Samuel could run and play. Our itinerary would take us next to Venice for Saturday and Sunday night, then on to Florence, where we had reservations for two nights just outside the city. From there we would go to one of our favorite places, Montalcino, since the boys were eager to show Sarah the castle there. We also planned to stay just outside of Todi because, as Samuel would often say, "Jody lives in Todi!"

It was a busy trip, filled with the constant talk and laughter that comes when seven relatives are together, three of them under the age of nine. But Bart kept his eye out for moments when he could still have me to himself. While in Venice, we all took a water taxi to the island of Murano, where we watched a glass-blowing demonstration. Benjamin, enthralled with the art there, tried to buy a glass turtle with the $10 we had given him for the day. The actual price of the piece was closer to $50, but the merchant agreed to give it to Benjamin for $10 because he was impressed that this American boy could speak Italian so well. Benjamin still expected to get change back from his $10, and when I noticed his sad expression I had to explain to him how he had just gotten an amazing deal.

While we stopped for a treat, Bart went off on his own to a couple of the other shops. When he came back, he pulled me aside with one of those looks that told me something good was in the works. "I think I just found the art piece for our ninth anniversary!" he gushed. Our May 8 anniversary was still weeks away, but Bart recognized that we were in an ideal location to find something we would treasure. He escorted me to the shop, and as soon as I entered I could see the beautiful pieces were definitely a higher quality than most artworks we had seen. He pointed to a stunning vase that had at least three different levels. The artist had blown some small pieces, and once those cooled he had blown other designs encompassing even smaller pieces. The vase glittered with specks of gold and many bright colors, giving the sense of looking at fish under blue water.

"I know it costs more than we planned to spend," Bart explained, "but don't you think it's going to be something special?"

Gazing into my husband's sparkling eyes, there was no doubt I would agree to the purchase. Before we left the shop, we also bought my mom a tall, thin clown piece. A few moments later, while she was kidding with the boys as we all waited for the water taxi to return, Bart stood on the dock with his arms engulfing me, his whole body seeming to merge with mine and making me feel so safe. As Bart looked into my eyes, we started talking.

"What do you think we'll be doing for our anniversary?" I asked.

"We should get away, just the two of us," Bart responded, "maybe to Positano—a special dinner for sure."

"Sounds wonderful," I answered. "Then how the heck are we going to top that for our tenth anniversary next year?"

Bart chuckled, remembering that after celebrating our fifth anniversary in Hawaii we had vowed that the celebration of our tenth anniversary would need to be off the charts. We had mentioned going to Paris as one possibility.

"Maybe we'll just have to come back to Italy for a visit," he said with a mischievous grin. I nudged him in the ribs.

Soon the water taxi came, and we all boarded to return to our luxurious Venice hotel rooms. Though it was wonderful for us all to be together again, I was still dreaming of the days ahead with Bart. The current plan was to stay in Italy through the summer and get back to Boise for the start of school, on which I had insisted. Knowing that many of the Micron crew in Avezzano had been asked to extend their work stints longer than initially agreed, I suspected that Bart and I might be having a debate about staying beyond August, but that was for another day. Right now I was remembering the plan we had for the upcoming summer. Our Boise neighbor Vicki and her adolescent daughter Sunny, who used to babysit the boys back home, had visited us in Italy soon after we arrived. Vicki had graciously told us that Sunny would love to come back by herself over the summer and serve as a part-time nanny for Benjamin and Samuel. I happily anticipated having long, playful days with my boys, then leisurely, romantic nights and occasional getaways with Bart—seemingly an ideal summer.

Mom and Jody went out to dinner alone on the second night in Venice. When they came back laughing, I asked them what was going on. Mom explained how she had thoroughly enjoyed the dish she had ordered and made a point to try to tell the waiter how much she had liked it. "It's the best meal I ever had," she said. The waiter just smiled. She wasn't sure exactly what she had eaten, but as she explained the black sauce and other features Bart grinned and said, "Shirl, that was squid ink." Now we were all laughing.

The next morning we asked for a water taxi to take us to the parking garage, where we would grab our rental car and head toward Florence. As we were riding in the water taxi, suddenly I noticed the taxi was dropping us off at the train station, when we had already paid the driver to take us to the parking garage farther away. I was tempted to set him straight, but I considered our family dynamics that had played out over the weekend. More than once I had been called "bossy" or "a know-it-all," and anyone who knows me can attest to the fact that, indeed, I like things done correctly—which usually means my way. So I chose to keep my mouth shut and wait for Bart to figure out that we were getting ripped off. When he finally did, we were all off the boat, with our bags, and the water taxi driver was rushing off to con another customer.

"Let's just walk," Bart said. I knew this was going to be a long walk on what was already becoming a very hot day and the kids wouldn't last. Again, though, I chose to keep my mouth shut, waiting for someone else to figure this out. By the time the parking garage was in view, we were all exhausted, hot, and thirsty. "I'll take Samuel and walk the rest of the way to the car while you all wait here," Bart added.

As I watched them walk away, I could not stop thinking how utterly handsome my husband was and how much I loved him. Once Bart and Samuel came back with the car, I leaned over when no one was within earshot and whispered, "I love you, Barton!" He smiled and kissed me.

As we drove away from the hustle and bustle of Venice, I realized the kids were fading. Samuel hardly ever took a nap, and I needed him to have a long one, preferably the whole three hours to Florence, which I knew would only be possible if he was fed. This time I spoke up about the need to stop for lunch. At first Bart said he preferred to keep going, but I insisted. So we stopped at the next auto grill, the closest thing to fast food in Italy, which I didn't favor for our family but which I knew would provide the kids with a quick lunch.

We got through lunch in a reasonable amount of time, by Italian standards anyway, and as we headed back to the car Bart asked me to drive. This was not unusual because I would typically do a lot of the driving on our excursions since it was hard for me to relax when someone else was driving. And Bart had been doing most of the driving on this long trip. But for some reason, at that moment I was struggling to keep my eyes open.

"Let me rest for a while," I said. "I'll be able to drive later."

"But you never sleep in the car," he replied. "Are you sure you can't drive?"

"I'm sorry, I just can't," I answered. "But I will later, I promise."

I wasn't the only one getting sleepy. Shortly after we got back on the autostrada, I tried to close my eyes briefly but soon opened them again, aware of how quiet everyone had suddenly become. I looked to my left and saw Mom asleep against the window, with Sarah asleep on her lap. Samuel, directly behind my mom, was asleep in his car seat. Benjamin, seated behind me, had also drifted off. Jody was in the front seat chatting with Bart.

I gazed at the side of Bart's face, paying particular attention to his hairline. I had been cutting my husband's hair, as well as the boys' hair, since we had come to Italy, and I had to admit I had done a pretty good job with Bart. "It's amazing how much he still takes my breath away," I said to myself.

Then I began to pray: *Dear Lord, please give me peace. The people I care most about in this world are in this car. Please protect us. I need to drive for Bart. Please let me sleep, just for...*

What I know about the next fifteen minutes is only what I have been told. The driver of a semi truck lost control, apparently swerving to avoid a US Army truck that had just clipped him. The semi truck crossed the median and whipped through the emergency turnaround. The median was too high for Bart to see it coming. He had perhaps one second to respond. In that instant, he had turned our minivan so that he would take the brunt of the crash himself and, hopefully, we would be spared. It was my husband's last loving gesture.

Chapter 9
The Unbearable Words
"They're All Gone"

THE FIRST WORDS I REMEMBER speaking in a hospital bed outside Bologna, as I pushed a doctor's hand away from my forehead, were "*Basta! Basta! Per favore, basta! Questo e male! Per favore!*" ("Stop, stop. Please stop. This is bad. Please stop!") The doctor was putting stitches in my forehead, and it hurt. Everything hurt. With tears in his eyes, the doctor said, "But I have to do this." Finally understanding that he was only trying to help, I lowered my arm and soon fell back into a deep sleep.

The next time I awoke was upon hearing my sister Jody scream, "They are all dead!"

I tried to turn toward her, but everything still hurt. "Jody, if they were dead I would know it," I explained, surprising myself with the calmness in my tone. "I don't feel them gone. It's not possible."

I called for the nurse and asked, "*Dove mia famiglia?*" ("Where is my family?")

"*Unaltra ospedale*" ("In a different hospital"), she replied. I prayed that they were not suffering as much as I was.

I have only blurry, snapshot images of what happened next: Jody being taken out of my room, my friends Jonathan and Sheri from Micron arriving, Wayne coming, too, someone handing me a phone and hearing my sister Sue on the other end, Wayne speaking words that were making no sense, and then hearing the same words from Sue: "I am so sorry, JA, but they're all gone."

I tried to process what she was saying, but I still didn't feel it, didn't believe it. My mind flashed to the gypsies we would see near the garage in Rome by the Spanish Steps, having heard that they would not only take money right out of your purse but also that they loved blond, blue-eyed boys and would sometimes take them away. Focusing again on what Sheri had said, I asked, "Are you sure, Sheri? Couldn't someone have taken them?"

Her eyes didn't break from mine. "No, I am sure," she said softly.

I still didn't feel it, couldn't accept the unbearable reality, but I then knew they were dead: Bart, Benjamin, Samuel, Mom, and Sarah. Everyone who had been in the car except Jody and me, the five most important people in my life, were gone.

At the time, I had no sense of how long I stayed in that Bologna hospital. Only years later was I able to piece together a rough timeline: The accident happened on March 25, the funeral for my five departed loved ones was held in Boise on April 13, and I had only been in Boise a couple of days before that. So I must have spent the better part of two weeks recuperating in the hospital not far from the accident site.

I learned later how Wayne and everyone in the Micron family, both in Italy and in Boise, had rallied my family and friends from back home and had flown many of them to Italy to be with Jody and me: Jody's husband Paul, of course; Sue and her husband Rusty; my brother Steve; Jody's friend Darcy; and my close friend Martha. They also drove Sister Carla up from Sacro Coure. To this day, I am deeply grateful for their loving support and attempts to comfort a woman who could not be comforted. But I remember almost nothing of what happened while I was with them. It must be true that our minds do not give us more than we can absorb because my mind has blocked out what I did, what I said, and how I felt in those first excruciating days.

One thing I do remember was hearing a voice in my right ear reminding me to "breathe, breathe." With six broken ribs and a broken collarbone, it hurt too bad to breathe. I just wanted that voice to stop. I wanted it all to stop.

Another, lighter memory: One morning Jody and I were waiting for our family and friends to arrive and, because it was late and we were restless, we decided we would escape to find coffee. I got in my wheelchair, and Jody pushed me as she hobbled along. Nurses tried to intercept us, but as they shouted their commands in Italian I pretended not to understand.

We made it to the café at the entrance of the hospital, grabbed our coffees, and were sitting outside enjoying the fresh air when our support team approached, laughing and saluting our brilliant escape.

What I don't remember of that time when my life as the one left behind began, others have filled in for me. Much of what I have learned from them only emerged recently while I was writing this book. For all those years in between, I didn't want to know. Following are some of their recollections:

> **Wayne:** I remember being a bit annoyed when I was pulled out of an important meeting to talk to Sergio, our site director, that day. I was thinking, what is it now: a union problem, an issue with the work schedules? Sergio told me he had received a phone call from the officer at the scene of a horrific accident north of Bologna. Bart, Benjamin, Samuel, and Jill's mom and niece did not survive. They wanted me to come immediately because the hospital staff would not tell Jill where Bart and her boys were. She had suffered a head injury and severe leg injury.
>
> On that long car ride to the hospital, I remember wishing I had never called Bart to come to work in Italy. I wondered how Jill and her sister had even survived. When I entered Jill's room, I could see that she was relieved, thinking finally someone would talk sense into these people and let her see her boys and Bart. When I told her the truth, she looked at me as if I were talking in a different language. Then the sparkle I had always seen in her eyes instantly disappeared.

Sister Carla informed me later that she was allowed to see the bodies and had asked me if I wanted to view them. Apparently, I had never even considered it, but I did ask her what she observed. She said they were crushed; a photo of the accident scene shows our vehicle crumpled up like it had just gone through a compactor. Benjamin was not as severely crushed as the others, but the blood coming out of his ears indicated he might have died from something more like shaken baby syndrome.

Sister Carla also shared with me a story about the moment Benjamin had said good-bye to her in Avezzano the day we were to leave on our trip to Venice and Florence. "The way he hugged me and held me," she explained, "it was as if he was saying good-bye forever." Did my oldest son have some kind of premonition, too? I wondered.

At the accident scene, Garza, the driver of the US Army truck, had immediately rushed toward the driver who had been tossed out of the semi truck, assuming we were all dead. Garza told our group at the hospital that when they found me at the accident scene my arm was reaching back as if to protect my boys. He also reported that I kept saying, "Bart, Bart, Bart," just as I did any time I was nervous and needed my husband to hold me. But he couldn't hold me this time, and he never would again.

The news was circulating quickly back home in Boise. My friend Kelly received a phone message from her brother Steve, who also worked at Micron, informing her that "something important had happened." When I called from the hospital and started to explain what had happened, she said simply, "I heard." I have no memory of calling her. Kelly would have been on a plane to Italy in a heartbeat if she hadn't been the mother of twin nine-month-olds.

My sister-in-law Lisa and Bart's brother Todd were on vacation in Cannon Beach, Oregon, at the time. Micron called their empty house in Idaho, and when they got no answer they sent police to knock on doors in the neighborhood until finally they found someone who knew where they had gone. When Todd and Lisa were reached in Oregon, they immediately drove up to Tacoma to try to console Bart's parents, Duane and LaVonne.

My friend Martha, whom I had drawn close to as a neighbor before we moved to Eagle, has been especially detailed in her eyewitness accounts of everything lost to memory.

Martha: Not long before the accident I had told Jill to call me on that particular day if she had time because it was the start of spring break. I was making dinner when the phone rang. I thought it was Jill. Instead, it was my mom telling me to turn on the TV news. When I flipped it on, I heard something about an accident and distinctly recognized the name Kraft. Since the report was ending I called the station for more details.

"Tune in at six," they said. When I watched at six, I saw footage of the wreck…it didn't even look like a vehicle. Then my eye caught a glimpse of something familiar. At Benjamin's birthday party, just before Jill's family left for Italy in June, we had given him a backpack with CDs for the flight to Italy. There was that same backpack lying on the grass near the crumpled car.

As the news trailed off, I was thinking of how we were Samuel's godparents. Did the boys suffer? The TV station called, asking for an interview. "No way!" I said. The phone rang again. This time it was Wayne at the hospital explaining how Micron was getting friends and family together to fly them to Italy and asking if I could come. I said yes, of course, and then he told me Jill was there and wanted to talk to me. I was startled and excited because I was imagining that coming out of that wreck she might be in horrible shape, maybe even brain dead. When I talked to her, she sounded surprisingly lucid. "They're all gone. Mom, too," she said, "and I need my mom more than ever."

As I learned much later, many of those initial news reports also mentioned that just days before our accident three American tourists had been killed when a truck crashed into their tour bus. It really was dangerous driving among the Italians. However, as the details about the accident emerged, we learned that the semi truck apparently had gone out of control because the driver had been struck by the US Army truck and that Garza, the man at the wheel of that truck, had not been driving safely. The driver of the semi truck had also been driving too fast. It would be years before liabilities would be sorted out from all of that.

While Wayne and our other friends at Micron were making the arrangements for folks from Boise to come visit us, Brian flew back to Italy from the States to be with me and help Wayne. The two of them, and so many others in Italy, did whatever they could to help Jody and me, including going back to the scene to look for our special vase that had been in the car, as Wayne has noted.

Wayne: Two days after the accident Jill told me about the vase she and Bart had bought the day before the accident. Of course, I just assumed it would have been smashed to pieces, but I told Jill we would look into it. We went back to the scene and looked and looked but couldn't find it. Then we happened to be talking to one of the officers who had first rushed to the scene, and he told us that he had found it! When he gave it to us, I was amazed to see that while some pieces inside had shattered, it was otherwise completely intact. It was a beautiful handmade vase that looked like fishes were swimming inside.

Today, ten years later, that vase has a prominent place in my mountain home in Idaho, a reminder of the loving times I spent together with Bart rather than the accident.

In the hospital, I was so badly injured that had it not been for the loss of my family and the need to get home to Boise I might have been kept there for months. I had suffered six broken ribs; a broken collar bone; a laceration of my left shoulder; a compound fracture of my left wrist, which, along with a slice across my left hand, made it impossible to move that hand for months; a cut from the top of my head to the back of my skull, which left a permanent scar; a crushed right leg, a shattered fibula, and broken tibia. The Italian doctors, who did everything they could for me, put a temporary apparatus on that leg to hold it together until I could get back to the States—a big steel rod on the outside with smaller rods connecting my leg to it, clear into the bone. The constant pain it caused would remain a part of my life until a new apparatus replaced it after I returned to Boise. I had one surgery in Italy and would have four more in Boise.

But those were just the physical injuries. At least they could be treated. The hole that cut across the center of my heart and reached to the depths of my soul would never be healed. I would never see my husband, my dear sons, my mother, or my niece again. No one around me could know what that loss meant, or how it felt, but if they could never really soothe me they could at least stand with me. Martha has told me much about how they tried to do that.

Martha: When we got to the hospital, the doc told us not to ask Jill a lot of questions. He said she may look like Jill but be prepared for her to be different. She was in the same room with Jody. When we all walked into the room, Paul ran right to Jody, who screamed, "I'm so sorry! I'm so sorry!" Then I walked over to Jill's bed. I wanted to hug her, but I didn't think she could take the physical pressure. She had already had that leg surgery and was in a halo. Jill reached out to me and said, "I just wanted to tell you how much I love you, and I'm so glad to see you." Then she kept saying, "They're gone, they're gone." Her bed was by a big picture window. She looked out the window, and I took her hand and said, "I love you, too. I'm so glad you're alive." Jill asked me about my own two children, and I thought of how my daughter Sara, after first hearing the news, had said, "You have to go be with Jill, Mommy."

The people at Micron told us to be prepared to stay for a week, but it was clear that Jill was in no condition to travel anytime soon. I went to the hospital every day. The night before Easter Jill asked me to spend the night with her. She talked a lot. She told me how much fun they all had been having those last few days before the accident, and the funny things the boys did with Sarah. She said she did remember after the crash screaming, "Bart! Bart! Bart!" But there was only silence in response. She remembered scraping blades of grass off her cheek. She couldn't see anybody, couldn't reach for anybody, and just felt the searing pain on her leg. As I combed her hair and lay in bed beside her, I felt so encouraged that she had her wits, and when she announced the next morning that she really needed a manicure because there was still blood in her nails, I rushed in to make it happen.

The hospital in Bologna wasn't exactly up to our standards. I remember one morning, while helping to take Jill down for X-rays, the elevator did not work. The whole building was filthy, and people were smoking in the ICU. We all wanted to get her out of there as fast as we could, even though it meant having that terrible contraption on her leg so she would be mobile enough for the trip. When the doctors were ready to discharge her, the Micron people made arrangements for Jill and Jody and all of us to fly home directly from Bologna. Jill had other ideas.

This is where my own memory kicks in. I clearly recall being told they were going to send me straight back to Boise. "No way," I said. "I need to see my home here in Italy one more time before I go. This is where I will always remember them. I need to spend one more night there. This was our home. The house in Eagle was to be our future home, and there is no future."

That idea created some obstacles. It was an eight-hour drive back to Avezzano, and I would need to ride the whole way in an ambulance. But I insisted, and our friends at Micron made it happen. Leaving the hospital, I felt like a little kid, scared and so alone.

"I'll ride with you, Squirt," Sue said. She probably didn't say "Squirt" but she used to call me that when I was little, and that's what I heard as it seemed comforting. As well as being afraid, I was also exhausted from not sleeping. In the hospital I had been in constant pain, and they hadn't been giving me much pain medication or sleeping pills. On that ambulance ride, I remember dictating to Sue Bart's, Benjamin's, and Samuel's obituaries, which would subsequently appear in the newspaper in Boise and other places back home. Before telling Sue what to write, I prayed: "Lord, speak through me so that everyone who reads this will get a glimpse of how wonderful they truly were." I wanted these obituaries to show how much they were loved. I needed everyone to know them as I had.

When we made it to our Avezzano house, I was wheeled out of the ambulance in a wheelchair and carried up the steps. A bed was made for me in the living room, but what I really wanted was to get upstairs to be in the boys' room one more time, and I begged to be taken there. My brother Steve, Brian, and Wayne finally figured out how to cart me up there, and I got to spend about twenty minutes, stopping first in the bedroom where Bart and I had shared some of the most wonderful times of our marriage. After gazing at our wedding book on the dresser, I moved on to the boys' bedroom. I picked up a few of their favorite storybooks and smelled their clothes, but I didn't have time to lie on their beds.

I also wanted to go up to the third-floor playroom, but according to my memory I was not able to do that. Martha told me later that I was carried up there and managed to retrieve a few toys and other things that belonged to Benjamin and Samuel.

I do remember the echoes I heard ringing throughout the house and my determination to show Sue and Steve, and Martha and the others, everything about our home and what it had meant to us: here's where Benjamin and Samuel would sneak into our bed almost every night, when I would feel too tired or too comforted by their quiet breathing to move them back to their bed...here's where we ate dinner together...here's where we spent an afternoon making origami...here's where the boys and I tried yoga for dummies...here's where Samuel couldn't stop running and slid into a new ceramic piece, and Bart and I couldn't stop laughing...here's where Bart would ask me to dance with him after the boys had gone to bed.

So many memories, yet I only had one night in my home before everything was shoved in boxes and shipped to my house in Eagle, which would not smell like family as this home did. I spent that last night in the spot they had set up for me in the living room, where I stared up at the ceiling remembering: Benjamin and Samuel taking a bath, Bart shaving, reading bedtime stories, laughing, singing. The echoes of my life with my family were deafening. And when I wasn't hearing them, I was left to silently wonder how on earth I could go on without them.

There was one more stop I had to make before getting on the plane bound for the United States—Sacro Coure. I needed to say good-bye to Benjamin's class and Samuel's class, to the kids at the orphanage, and to the sisters.

Sister Carla already had given me a memory book the children and the sisters had made for Benjamin and Samuel. Across the Winnie the Pooh cover was written: "*Per un grande c vorr c: vuole un grosso abbraccio*" ("For a big heart, a gigantic kiss [or hug]")! The inscription read: "Benjamin and Samuel, be sure that your friends will never forget you and your wonderful family. Thanks for all you have been to us!" Hearts surrounded the book's border. The school principal, Sister Elisabetta, had inscribed to Benjamin: "I wrote you in heaven." Inside, the children had created beautiful drawings to go with class photos. Each child also had written words in Italian that Sister Carla had thoughtfully translated into English. So much love poured from them. I managed to stick with the page Sister Carla had written for Benjamin long enough to read:

> *My little Benjamin, it is so hard for me to realize what happened to you, to your little wonderful brother Samuel, to your dad, Sarah, and grandma...no answers...just lot of questions, but I do believe God will show us everything at the right time....I know for sure you are in heaven, with God, and I know for sure you are holding your wonderful mom's hand so that she can keep walking...she still has so much to give....And you were like her. Do you remember your nicknames? Water Melon Cheek (you loved it so much!). My little Koala (you used to jump on my legs singing with your sweet voice)....All of these names are close to my heart. Your ways were so delicate! What a wonderful boy—I thank God because of you and your family! You made a difference in my life, and I will always bring you close to my heart. Now, Benjamin, please listen to my prayer: all that I ask you now is to be close to your Mommy. She needs you now more than ever, so, honey, please ask God to keep her close to his heart so that she can rest and find the peace she really needs. You are invisible, Benjamin, but you are there. So help her to not give up, help her to understand that she can make a difference in people's lives....Guide her toward God, she'll understand his plans in her life. Be her angel. With Sarah, Samuel, Daddy, and Grandma. Amen. Thank you, my special boy—you know how much I loved you, and I will be forever...Sister Carla.*

While I was still in the hospital in Bologna, the Sisters of Sacro Coure and the Micron employees arranged a funeral in Avezzano for people there who had known and loved Bart and the boys. I was fortunate to have obtained a video of the event, and amid all the smoke from the incense and the Italian prayers in the formal Catholic Mass, I could clearly recognize the faces of the kids from Benjamin's school and their parents. A girl and a boy from Benjamin's class spoke, and then all the kids formed a line and, one by one, laid flowers on the memorial. I wished I had been able to attend, or that Sister Carla could have told stories about what made Bart,

Benjamin, and Samuel so special. Still, it is meaningful to watch, even today, because those Italian people were part of my family, our family. Avezzano was home.

Now I had to find the strength to show those children that although bad things happen life goes on, and that they would be okay and I would be okay. They had shown so much love for all of us, and I needed to let them know how much my boys loved them.

In Benjamin's classroom, Sister Carla translated for me as I tried to reassure the children that this tragedy would not ruin their lives. I taught them "I love you" in sign language, which had always been Benjamin's favorite. As I finished and someone wheeled me to Samuel's classroom, I was surprised to find the hallway lined with parents and townspeople clapping for me in a universal language of love and support. At Samuel's classroom, Sister Pasquina greeted me in her familiar coarse voice, saying, "*Ti voglio bene!*" I smiled, remembering how even when Samuel would not believe she was saying, "I love you," he would always take the candy she would offer before rushing away out of arm's reach.

After talking to Samuel's preschool class, I headed upstairs to the orphanage. I knew this would be the most difficult good-bye. These kids had enough bad in their lives. They needed to feel love from me, from the boys, and from God. I had someone go to a store in Avezzano and buy crosses made in Murano for the children. I gave one to each of them, and in return I received a hug and a kiss.

Then it was time to drive to Rome to fly to the United States. My family and friends who had come all the way from Boise and stayed two weeks to be with me were now ready to escort me back. Micron had purchased at least two rows of first class seats for our group. But I had one more loving supporter in my brigade. Sister Carla had obtained permission from the mother superior of Sacro Coure to come back to Boise with me. This special woman, who as far as I knew had never left Italy or even flown on an airplane, was putting aside her life at the orphanage and the school for two weeks to be at my side in faraway Boise, Idaho. Our connection meant that much to her. There are no words to explain how deeply this touched me, except to say that I believe I could not have left Italy without her. I needed to return with someone from my life in Italy because I was going to Boise without my family—just as my premonition had indicated.

Chapter 10
The Question
Why Am I Here?

WHAT I EXPERIENCED during my first few days in Boise was recorded in the following journal entry.

We land in Boise, and I can't wait to get past security. No, I'm not thinking of all my family and friends waiting to greet Jody and me. I'm focused only on the pain pills I had called ahead for my doctor to prescribe and for my sister-in-law Mary to have waiting for me. As I am being wheeled closer to the doors, I see my stepfather Dick. He is grieving the loss of his wife. As we make eye contact, I can't hold back the tears. "I love you, Dick, and I am so sorry!" I say. And this man who has always tried so hard to control his emotions envelops me in a hug.

I look toward Mary and ask for the medication. She didn't pick it up; she didn't know I needed it now. I tell her I understand, but inside I am struggling to contain myself and want to blurt out: "I can't do it anymore... please take the pain away! Please, I can't handle it. I'm not this strong. Lord, please!"

The next hours and days are a haze. Too many people coming in and out of the house. The phone ringing thirty or forty times a day: What do I need? What can they do to help? Here's a book that might help.... Then Sue is telling me I have to go to the viewing. Not only that, she wants me to go before it starts so I can have my own time with them before the others arrive. I don't want to go. Again I want to scream: "Don't you understand—everyone is fucking dead! I can't, I don't have the strength to deal with this. When is this going to end? Please let it end!!"

I agree to go only when Sue promises me Tablerock chicken bites and, of course, a beer. I enter the viewing room in Summers Funeral Home...those little caskets...could my boys really be in there? And that one, where my soul mate is…why did he leave me? He promised. I want to shout to him: "Please don't make me do this alone, Bart. Bart, I need you….Please don't leave me! Why did you leave me?"

The public viewing begins. With Sister Carla on one side of my wheelchair and Kelly on the other side, I do my best to keep it together enough to greet everyone, even though I can barely remember my own name, let alone the dozens here trying to show me their love. One woman I don't know starts whispering in my ear that she understands. I want to shake her and yell at her, "No, you don't understand! No one understands!! Leave me alone!!!" I direct Kelly to get her away from me, and as I look up there is Bart's close friend from Boise watching. "I'm sorry, I'll leave," he mutters. I say, "No, Pete, it's not you. Please stay." So much confusion all around me…

My eyes detect a group of people who some voice inside tells me I know very well. I look at them closely and realize I have no idea who they are, and they are getting closer. "They are your family from Oklahoma," Kelly whispers in my right ear, just in time. It's my Aunt Dean, an amazingly strong woman whom I love very much. She was planning to visit us in Italy in the spring. "I am so sorry," I want to tell her. "I'm so sorry we ruined your trip to see us. I am so sorry."

My pain and confusion did not let up the next day at the burial and funeral. In the morning before the service, I was wheeled across the lawn on a ride so bumpy I was afraid that I might get thrown out of my wheelchair or that it would tip over. Seeing Brian and Wayne gave me strength enough not to yell at being the focus of everyone's pitying eyes. As I eyed the five caskets, two big and three little, I wanted to run away and escape this hell. My skin was crawling, and I still wanted to scream at the top of my lungs when suddenly I was snapped out of my thoughts by the sound of real screaming. My nephew Jack, who was only five, was being directed to kiss each casket and say good-bye to his grandma and cousins—his best friends. I told my brother Steve, "Get him out of here now!" I wanted to protect Jack, to make it okay for him, and I couldn't.

We entered the Bishop Kelly High School gymnasium. Hundreds of people were there, and it seemed they were all staring at me, waiting to see if I was going to crack. Sister Carla held my hand. "It's all right," she whispered. "You are going to be okay." I wanted to believe her.

The funeral opened with the song "Somewhere Over the Rainbow" played to a photo montage of all of them. Seconds later I was looking at a photo of Samuel with birthday cake smeared all over his face and the words "Angels Among Us." I swallowed.

Others who had the strength that I lacked stood up to speak. Jody's husband Paul spoke lovingly about his daughter Sarah. Benjamin's godparents, Jody and Steve Cecil, spoke of his amazing ability to love. Martha described Samuel as "a ball of energy—a fun-loving, candy-loving sweetheart." Sue explained Mom's "oh happy day" presents. Todd shared his memories of Bart. I caught only a few words now and then, especially how Bart would often thank God for "the three angels in his life." I knew Todd was speaking from his heart, and he added his gracious prayers for me, but as I watched him I just kept wishing that I could be up there. I would have told them all something like this: "Bart was my soul mate, and Benjamin and Samuel were my life. Our relationships were so loving, so close. Sarah was like a daughter to me. My mom was my best friend. They were my life!"

But even if I had summoned the nerve to get up there and had gotten that far with my remarks, I would have been tempted to add this: "And there is no way I should be here. God meant for me to die, too. It's a mistake!" That probably would not have gone over well at a memorial service for five people who had touched hundreds of adults and children in our community.

A disconcerting interlude during the funeral service occurred when all of a sudden some man I didn't know got up to give the eulogy, saying that he was the pastor of my church. I had asked for Pastor Mark from my church, The Community of Life, to deliver the eulogy, but instead I was listening to a stranger who didn't know my family. Then he said what in my state sounded like the stupidest thing anyone could say, something like, "If you think this is bad, you should see how many other people are suffering in Third World countries around the globe." I looked at Sister Carla, who glanced back at me in confusion, wondering if she had understood correctly.

That's when I got the giggles. How could anything get any worse? People were staring at me, kids crying, a stranger speaking nonsense, everyone who mattered most in my life was being buried and all I could do was sit there helpless in my wheelchair. I couldn't stop laughing, probably as a substitute for torrents of tears. I plugged my nose, but it didn't help. Sister Carla elbowed me, which only made my giggles worse. What I actually wanted to say, instead of giggling, was, "I'm done! I cry uncle, Lord. Get me fucking out of here! Stop my fucking life!"

At the reception, held in downtown Boise at The Grove, I told people whatever I thought they wanted to hear: "I'll be okay...I have family and friends surrounding me, and God will see me through this....I'll rely on him....They are in a better place." If I had been given truth serum, I would have said something more like, "If you keep giving me wine, maybe I'll make it through this god-awful day."

The following days didn't get any better. At least Sister Carla remained with me for a couple of weeks in that big, lonely house in Eagle, giving me a sense of peace and calm. I relied on her so much that when she left the room I would panic. With Sister Carla, I could be honest. Around her, I could even laugh. She would tease me by holding up one of my wine bottles and saying, "Jill, you drink too much wine." I remember the day she was pushing me in the wheelchair around Eagle in the rain, and as we both were getting soaked she took off her habit and put it on me, making us both laugh.

Eventually, she invited me to call her Carla, to drop the sister title, and shared with me more about her own life. She told me the story of when she knew her calling in life was to become a nun. She also revealed her desire to have a place in the mountains where she could teach people how to pray and worship to face life's challenges, as well as share her love of music. I imagined her having a retreat center where she was able to assist many people like me.

With Carla I could ask the real questions of my life: How do I get through another day? How can I not be angry with God? How can I love anyone? How can I trust anyone or anything? She had no answers, but she gave me the gift of understanding my pain without judging me, something I felt was too difficult for those in my family who were so wrapped up in their own grief that the depth of my pain was too much for them to fathom.

When Carla went back to Sacro Coure, I felt practically helpless, barely able to shower or go to the bathroom by myself. Family and friends did step up, often staying with me for days or weeks at a time. I needed them but also felt frustrated when they would tell me what I "should" do. For several weeks, I couldn't even keep food down. When my mother-in-law LaVonne came to take care of me for a while, she would ask me to eat a couple of crackers every time I awoke during the night, then greet me with a shake of fruit and yogurt each morning. Eventually, they convinced me to meet a therapist named Sharon Katz, which I believed was a waste of time. "They are dead," I said to myself, "and no amount of talking about it is going to bring them back." But I allowed Sharon to come to the house a few times a week to visit with me, just to get my family and friends off my back. She just listened to me—a woman who could barely function, let alone start the grieving process.

It seemed puzzling to me how the outside world kept turning, even though my own world had stopped. I couldn't figure out how to deal with daily tasks and money matters, but my sister-in-law Lisa was helpful in organizing my life, making sure I made appointments and paid bills. Lisa also provided perspective on my behavior at the time.

Lisa: Since our homes in Eagle were very close, Jill would often ask me to come over to be with her. It was hard for her to see Todd because he reminded her too much of Bart, but she did call on me to help her pay her bills, change the names on statements sent to Bart and Jill, change the caller ID so callers didn't see Bart and Jill on the other end. Things like that. I was at her house almost every day for a while. I'd help her with breakfast, and if I was there for lunch I would try to make sure she ate something, though she never ate much. She would repeat stories about Bart and her boys over and over. Sometimes they were in her dreams, and she did not want to wake up. She would say, "I can feel them, I can hear them."

When Sister Carla was still there, I could see what a big help she was to Jill. When I would visit the two of them, Sister Carla was so gracious—she would offer to leave the room if Jill and I needed private space. One night Jill called me and said, "The lights went out, and I can't get the flashlight." When I arrived, Sister Carla was there, without her habit. After an initial moment of embarrassment, she said, "It's okay, it's only you." Everyone who met Sister Carla really liked her. I belong to the King of Glory Lutheran Church, and one of our woman pastors came over just to meet her. Sister Carla understood what was happening. She was very worried about how fragile Jill was. She would say, "People don't have this type of grief, where you just lose everyone in your life all at once." As the days went on, I knew Jill was really struggling.

Indeed, I was really struggling. I had a hard time completing a sentence, and I couldn't focus sufficiently to follow a conversation, a television show, a movie, even read. I couldn't remember events from ten minutes before, let alone the day before. Was I losing my mind? Would I ever be the same? Did I even care? People were phoning and trying to help, but they would ask me such questions as Did you eat? Take a shower? Clean your injured leg? Would you like to see a movie? What kind of music do you want? Could I visit? What do you really need? Can we do anything? I felt as though I would explode at any moment, but I had no idea why. I had no idea what to tell them since I didn't know how to answer their questions, let alone come up with anything I needed or wanted. All I knew was what was going on in my heart: "I just want to escape. I just want to be with my boys. Bart, I need you! Mom, what am I supposed to do? I don't know what to do. I don't know what I need. I don't know where I am. Please, just take me away. Just make me numb. Please! I am losing my mind!"

When people were around me, they were often so scared to say the wrong thing they would not even mention their own kids or spouses. When they did dare to recall any memory of my family, it would usually pertain to things that happened at least one year prior to the accident, before we had left Boise. Yet almost all the vivid memories I carried with me sprang from that last year with them in Italy. So we just didn't connect. Martha's reflection on the time helps portray the feelings I was expressing at the time.

> **Martha:** I stayed over in Jill's home in Eagle with her many nights. She didn't sleep much, so sometimes I would sleep in bed with her to help. I said to myself, "When people leave and it gets quiet, she's going to need me more than ever." Sometimes she was incredibly angry at Bart. Other times she was angry at her mom. She would ask, "How could they leave me? Why am I here?" I would say, "Who knows why? There is some reason, but we may not know it for a long time. I'm just so glad that you are here." But then, on my drive home, I would think about why she really didn't want to be here. After a while Jill pulled away from me. It was just such a hard time.

When I could manage to get out to go shopping and do other errands, I often faced an even more painful dilemma. When people recognized me from reading about the news of the accident in the paper, they would often point and whisper. The brave ones came up to talk to me. If someone who didn't recognize me would start asking me about my life, it would usually begin with the two most agonizing questions: "Are you married? Do you have kids?"

What could I say? I felt trapped. I would usually mumble something like, "I was married, but my husband is dead," and then, in hopes of comforting me, they would then ask if we had children. "I had two boys: Benjamin six and Samuel four. They are dead, too." Then I would have to deal with their shock and sadness, as well as having my own painful feelings stirred. The alternative was worse. If I lied and said I didn't have a husband or kids, I would have felt I was betraying their memory. I could never do that!

Many times the person asking questions would feel obliged to keep talking rather than just walk away in shock, compounding my quandary. They'd say, "Do you have your mom and dad around?" And I would say,

"No, my mom died in the accident, too, and my dad suffered a serious stroke." At that point, I'd want to throw up. If they kept at it, I would mumble something like, "I appreciate your thoughts and prayers," before quickly trying to complete any errand, driving home, crawling into bed, and turning on the TV. Even that was not much of an escape since it seemed like every movie I'd start watching would show some loved one dying or some other tragedy.

The following exchange, which I had with the woman seated next to me when I flew to Michigan to visit Aunt Doris, exemplifies what I would often go through when people asked questions about my life circumstances:

"Are you married?"

"No, I lost my husband in a car accident."

"How horrible! Do you have any children?"

"No, I lost them in the accident, too."

"I'm so sorry. Do you have family to help you deal with your loss?"

"Mom died in the accident, and Dad's in assisted living."

"Oh, my God! What do you do then? I mean, do you have a job?"

"I do a lot of journaling, see a lot of doctors, and have a massage once a week."

To this woman, and to many others who asked such questions, I never found the strength to blurt out what I *really* wanted to tell them: "Shut the hell up! I'm not doing well. I have no one. I can barely breathe or get out of bed. I don't have the energy to calm you down right now, and I really don't want to talk about it. I don't want to be a freak show. Yet I don't know how not to tell you, how to not think about it every second of every day. And all of this is none of your goddamn business!"

My physical injuries also were taking their toll. I had surgery to take the old apparatus off my right leg and put on a new one, which I named Beatrice. When the doctors attached Beatrice to me, they put some plates in my leg and foot and a brace on my ankle to help me walk. This new apparatus had four halos and seventeen pins, some screwed into a nut that is still connected to my bone. Wearing the apparatus, my clothes and bedsheets tore on a daily basis. Once I could walk I had to be careful not to gouge my left leg with it. Naming the apparatus Beatrice helped me cope with having it as a part of me for so long because the name was associated with one of the few lighter moments I experienced in those days. Some college friends were visiting me at that time, and I was about to meet my friend Jim's new girlfriend, Zeke. When I asked my friend Steve what Zeke's real name was, he told me it was Beatrice. To his embarrassment, it turned out that he had the name wrong—it was actually Michelle. For some reason I found this funny, and that's when I decided to name my new apparatus Beatrice. Steve had given me the ability to have a sense of control over the contraption.

I had to clean Beatrice with hydrogen peroxide and Q-tips twice a day. I had to push the skin, which seemed to grow much faster than I could keep up with, back down around each pin. The part that caused the most pain was when my foot had to be strapped onto the apparatus so my ankle would bend. This created a dull ache that penetrated up my leg. And I was expected to sleep like that! Oh well, I wasn't sleeping anyway.

A few times my leg became infected, causing pain I can't describe except to say that it was hot to the touch and led to skyrocketing fevers. Meanwhile, it took intense physical therapy to get the movement back in my hand. I never knew that squeezing a ball could hurt so much and how important it was not to allow the scar tissue to adhere to the ligaments. I also needed surgery on my neck. It was causing my good arm to tingle and at times go numb, and the doctor told me that even if I only tripped and fell, it could cause me to become paralyzed. This led to more plates and screws.

If there was any positive element in what I was going through, it was that at least I did not have to overly fret about finances. Bart and I had saved for our future. In my childhood, we didn't even talk about money, and when I was first married I couldn't balance a checkbook. Bart, however, insisted that we plan ahead "in case something happened to him." It was one of the many ways my husband's love stayed with me. Another way Bart stayed with me was through his wedding ring. When I buried Bart, I wasn't emotionally able to put his wedding ring on his finger. I wasn't sure why; I just sensed that I needed it more than he did. That first summer I figured out what to do with it. I had a band made with

Benjamin's and Samuel's birthstones and had it soldered onto Bart's ring to make a tangible and beautiful reminder of all of them. I still wear it today.

And Bart stayed with me in still another way. His financial planning ultimately allowed me to make what would turn out to be a very healthy move to begin a new life after the accident. After finding myself walking through empty room after empty room in our big Eagle house, seeing belongings in big boxes sent over from Italy that I could find no reason to unpack, I decided I would build my own home to start anew. This decision was made easier by a fortuitous encounter with the contractor who had built our Eagle home. One day, as I was walking my Dalmatian dog Cinder, I ran into this contractor, Peter, who said, "Jill, you find a piece of property anywhere in the Boise area and I will build you a home." So I set off to do just that! Working with Peter enabled me to feel that I was somehow bringing along a piece of the house Bart and I built together, as well as a little of the Italy home, while creating a new environment I could call *my* home and that would be my safe haven, Putting the Eagle house up for sale was a relief. The only problem was I could not stand one more night surrounded by the future I lost. I would need to live in an apartment during the sale of the house in Eagle and the construction of the new one. However, I soon discovered that if the house in Eagle tormented me with its emptiness, the apartment engulfed me with its darkness. I was taking a ton of meds: for depression, for anxiety, for sleeping, for pain, but only took pills for depression and sleeping on a regular basis. In order to sleep a couple of hours at night, I took five or six Ambien a day. And I admit that I also sought to diminish my pain with alcohol. Logically I knew that drinking so much was only adding to my depression, but it helped me feel somewhat numb for short respites, which I needed.

After losing a good deal of weight from not eating when I first came home, I gained it all back and much more when I was able to eat again. Going grocery shopping was a confusing and painful reminder of my loss since I had to learn how to go from cooking for four to cooking for one and how to eat meal after meal at an empty table instead of with babbling, laughing children and an engaged husband. My body became fat and ugly since I filled myself up with junk food just to occupy my time and was unable to exercise due to my injuries. For a while I even became bulimic in an effort to control my weight. When I was vomiting, I looked as ugly as I felt on the inside.

My state of confusion also persisted, causing me additional anxiety. I continued to have moments, even whole nights, when I could not remember where I was or what I was doing. I finally learned from Sharon, my therapist, that this was called dissociating, a common result of trauma that works as a coping mechanism. As a result of dissociating, many details of that first year after the accident have been lost to my memory, making it necessary to turn to others to bring back what I have been unable to retain. Looking back at that time now, I can see that I was stuck trying to sort out the answer to a question I could not articulate: How does one mourn alone? I knew that people loved me, including my family. But they were all hurting so bad, and they just didn't know what to do. They needed to find their own way to grieve, and I needed to find mine. Consequently, we clashed more than we connected. So being around me during this time made most people too sad or uncomfortable to offer me the emotional support I desperately needed. My family and friends would try to understand me, and some believed they did. Yet all too often their urge to help made me feel as though I was being pressured to move on. What they seemingly couldn't understand was that each person's grief is very different and only the grieving person can truly access what is necessary to do. The grief of losing a mother is different from the grief of losing a father. The grief of losing a spouse is different from the grief of losing a child. And the grief of losing a child is different with each of the individual children you lose. I lost them all. I could not and was not moving on. I was hardly moving at all. I felt like a burden and that it would have been easier for all if I had just died also.

I couldn't even find a way to connect with Jody, though we both had come out of that crash alive and both suffered injuries and loss. When she talked about losing Sarah, it would hurt me so much. And I am positive that if I talked to her about Benjamin or Samuel, which I don't really remember doing, it must have crushed her. Jody had to deal with many painful obstacles of her own. Among other things, she had to prove she had a head injury because she did not have the ability to work full-time. Picturing myself in her position, I couldn't imagine having to go to work and put on a front, and then on top of that have people ask questions about the accident and her well-being.

The image I held of myself was as a giant, oozing, pussy wound. Even Cinder was getting depressed being around me. She was hardly eating, and sleeping all the time, not exactly the norm for a Dalmatian. I decided it was best for both of us to give her away so she could live in a place where she could run and play. That was another tough decision, adding further loss.

It was so difficult to connect with people and overcome my depression that from time to time I would find myself believing I wasn't going to be around much longer. If I really had survived for a reason, as everyone insisted, then all I had to do was fulfill whatever purpose I had been given and then surely God would allow me to join my family. Only it wasn't happening fast enough. My journal entries remind me of that frustration, and of my anger about what happened, my anger at my family, and my anger at God:

> *May 28, 2002: Why, God, did I have to stay? This is so much for anyone to take! Bart was my love. We had so much in common, and we shared everything. Benjamin and Samuel were my world. They were so loving, kind, and creative. I think about their soft cheeks rubbing against mine. Their laughter and smiles. Their hugs and kisses. How I loved holding their little hands and cuddling before they fell asleep and the smell of them....I want so badly to hold them again and wake from this nightmare!*
>
> *What am I going to do? My life is meaningless! I keep thinking if only things had somehow been different that day leaving Venice. If we would have left earlier, or not stopped for lunch....It seems too unreal. How on earth could I be going through my worst nightmare and not have Bart by my side? I know he turned the car so it would hit on his side, and that is what saved Jody and me. I wish so bad he would have let me go, too!*

August 8, 2002: *I want so badly to end my life. And I would—if God could guarantee that I would be with them.*

A month later I was granted a brief reprieve from my grief. I decided to return to Avezzano for a visit and a more proper good-bye. In Italy, I could remember Bart, Benjamin, and Samuel's faces again! Our friends Max and Cay from Micron were going back to Italy and would move into our former Avezzano house, so I had travel companions. For two weeks, I would get to live with my happy memories of our family's nine months in Italy.

That is actually what occurred. Being in Italy also brought me back to Sister Carla. She took me to the Vatican and introduced me to one of her favorite places near Rome: Santa Maria della Concezione dei Cappuccini, Our Lady of the Conception of the Capuchins, otherwise known as "The Church of the Bones." The crypt there enshrines the skeletal remains of four thousand Capuchin friars. The bones are nailed to the wall in distinct patterns, including a cross and a clock, in what was established in the 1600s as a silent reminder of the swift passage of life on earth. Before we returned to Avezzano, I took Sister Carla to the Hard Rock Café. It was comforting to be with her again, although from the moment of the accident she had never been at all distant from me. After her two-week stay in Boise in April, she had maintained a strong presence through phone calls and letters. I remember once she wrote that "Benjamin was born with your heart. You were twins in your hearts." And I cried because it was true: I'd look in Benjamin's eyes and I would see my own.

Carla also would tell me over and over that God was on my side. Of course, *that* was a lot harder to accept as truth! "Someday you will find yourself changed and will recognize God's hand," she wrote. "God can't take away the pain from your heart. He'll give you strength, though. Suffering is a mystery, and there are no answers. Face it, not by yourself but with God."

Additionally, Carla revealed to me what the depth of our friendship meant to her personally, writing, "God waited and waited to send me a gift, and finally he sent you to me! This experience has changed me so much.

I won't be the same anymore." Then I would wonder: Did I even deserve such a gift as Carla was to me?

This feeling of being undeserving of close friendships—no doubt because of my loss—also transferred to others. I wondered whether I deserved the unwavering love and support from my dear friend Kelly, with whom I had been friends since third grade. We had gotten to know each other because she had had a crush on my older brother Steve. Kelly and I would go to the canal, where she would show me how to catch crawdads. We made forts in the field where her grandparents lived with horses, goats, chickens, and calves. Later, Kelly's daughter Sadie was born nine months after Benjamin. I took care of Sadie for a couple of months when she had colic. When Kelly's husband Jeff got a job transfer with the state Fish and Game Commission just a few months before our family was to move to Italy, Kelly was pregnant with twins. I invited her to live with us in our Eagle home, and her twins Colton and Carley were born the day after we left. When I first returned after the accident, her family was living a good distance away in Stanley, so Kelly couldn't see me that often. But when I reached out to her, she was always there, as she described in a later reflection about those days.

> **Kelly**: I made some emergency trips from Stanley, about three hours away, to see Jill when she was having a hard time. She called me on my birthday, and I could tell she was crying. "Do you need me?" I asked. "Yes," she said. So I drove to get to her as soon as I could. That apartment she was living in was so bleak, so dark, and she was so lonely there. Whenever I went to see her, I would just listen to her. She'd keep saying, "I just miss them so much." I didn't know how she'd make it.

My first Christmas was hell. I didn't want to let my nieces and nephews down and not get them presents, but the toy store was too overwhelming. A friend whom I had known before I met Bart told me that he would help. I explained to him that although I knew he had a crush on me, I had no interest in him. "I need to surround myself with people I can trust. I am drinking a lot, and when I get drunk I get very flirtatious. I miss Bart's arms around me so much, and I cannot be around people who don't understand," I told him. He reassured me that he understood my situation and only wanted to help. We headed to the mall a couple of days before Christmas. With every present I bought, we stopped for a celebration drink. I remember being in some parking lot with Kelly giving me the Christmas present she had bought me and thinking I should be more sober for this. I remember the aching for my boys that would not go away no matter how much I drank. Then I don't recall anything else until I woke up nauseous and naked next to the man, and knowing I had screwed up. Why had I let my guard down? On top of this man's betrayal, I felt the sadness of not having Bart there to protect me.

My family decided to rent a place up at Bogus Basin for the holidays, where they could ski and I could watch; they could enjoy the hot tub, and I could watch since I still had Beatrice on. I watched the kids play but did not know how to communicate with them. Their touch became excruciatingly painful because my heart ached so badly for my own boys. One morning I was awakened to the sound of my dad crying. He had had an accident, and someone needed to clean him. Because everyone was having such a hard Christmas, I quietly did what was needed so the others didn't have to wake up. The next day Dad had to be taken to the hospital. He was talking nonstop and was incoherent and seemingly delusional, at one point believing he was talking to Samuel. "Why is no one helping Samuel? Can't you hear him crying?" he asked.

Not even finally getting Beatrice removed from my leg slowed my downward spiral. On February 12, about six weeks before the first anniversary of the accident, I was in my apartment, alone, having a bottle of wine. As I was heading to bed, I decided to take my sleeping pills. I opened the bottle, and, somehow, all twenty-five pills poured into my hand. I stared in the mirror at the image of the ugly woman that was like a giant pussy wound.

"Fuck it!" I said, slamming all the pills in my mouth. Confused, I thought I experienced falling to the floor, but I know that I didn't. I wasn't really sure that I had just taken twenty-five pills but wondered what I should do if I had. Then I thought of how much my family and friends were worried about me, and I decided I had better take all the pain pills in the drawer. "This way they wouldn't have to be concerned about me anymore, and I'll get to be with my family at last," I said to myself.

I lined the bottles up so no one would have to do an autopsy. And then I lay in bed, just waiting. Suddenly another thought occurred to me: *A note! Didn't most people write a note?* So I got up to write one. I told everyone who mattered most to me how much I loved them and urged them to move forward and not allow this to ruin their lives. I explained why they were special in my life, what they had done to bring me joy and happiness, and how they had helped me. Feeling satisfied, I lay down again. Then I had yet another thought: *Martha! I forgot to mention my friend Martha.* Not wanting to hurt her by squeezing her into the note as an afterthought, I reached for the phone.

"I drank a bottle of wine so that is why I am slurring," I tried to explain. Martha's later reflection on my suicide attempt describes the circumstances I could not recall.

> *Martha*: Jill sounded so casual at first: "Hey, how are you doing? How are things going? I'm just hanging out here." I said, "Are you sure you're okay? Would you like me to come over?" but she just said, "No, I'm just going to bed early…but I guess if you wanted to get together…." I knew something was not right, so I told my husband Bob I needed to go right away.
>
> When I got there, Jill was in bed, with two empty wine bottles beside her. "I took some pills," she said. I jumped up and ran to the bathroom. There was one bottle on each side of the counter, both empty. "Is that what you took? How many?" I asked. "Oh, I don't know," she said. I looked at the prescription date and noted it was just a week ago. "Did you take a lot of these?" I asked. "Well, some spilled." I should have called 911 right away, but all I could think of was to contact my sister in Nevada because she's a nurse. When I told her that I thought Jill took several pain pills with Tylenol, she said, "Martha, hang up and call 911!" I didn't even know the address of Jill's apartment. I just tried

to describe the apartment complex and told the police I would watch for them outside.

"Jill, you took an overdose. We're getting you help," I said. "But that's not why I asked you to come," she insisted. I found her suicide note when I was looking for something with her address on it. It said something like: "I'm sorry, but you know why I can't stay. I just want to be with my boys...." In the hospital, Jill kept telling everyone, "You don't understand! I don't want to be here!"

When I woke up in the hospital, I felt quite different, and not just from having my stomach pumped. For the first time in eleven months I actually wanted to live! When the hospital released me, the law required me to be kept in a psychiatric hospital, which was a horrible experience. To me, it seemed like the other patients there didn't know what pain was and that not even the counselor could grasp what I was going through. They just made me draw my "happy picture," which seemed ridiculous. When the lady across the room said, "See, I am lying here, and these hearts are raining down on me..." I thought, "My God, I am going to have to jump across this room and strangle her!" I was overwhelmed by the stench of cigarette smoke since the door to my room was next to the one that opened to the smoking area. Also the door to the bathroom would not lock, so one never knew if the other three "inmates" would barge in. At one point I remember talking quietly to Peter on my cell phone, answering important construction questions and trying hard not to reveal to him where I was. I spent one night in that facility before my therapist Sharon arranged to get me out.

This experience of attempting suicide had been a wake-up call, and now I knew I had a choice: the road of misery, which no one could blame me for following, or some kind of happiness—some new road I couldn't imagine but had to believe was out there.

And I knew where I needed to be if I were really going to have a chance to begin living again. Sacro Coure was calling me back.

Chapter 11
The Convent

SOON AFTER I HAD BEEN RELEASED from the hospital I had called Sister Carla and explained what had happened. "I need a place to stay for a while where I can get my head on straight," I said, hesitatingly. "Something tells me that Italy is the right place. So I was wondering if I could stay in . . . well, in the convent?"

"Of course you can stay with us, Jill," she replied. "I will work it out. God wants you to be here." Once again my trusted friend, who happened to be a Catholic nun, had been able to just listen, without judging, as she had always done, and offer support.

To prepare for my visit with the sisters of Sacro Coure, I stopped in a Christian bookstore in Boise. I closed my eyes and prayed for God's guidance in leading me to some kind of guide to grief recovery that would help me take the next critical step in my healing. When I opened my eyes, I was staring at *Grief Recovery Workbook* by Chaplain Ray Giunta. As I glanced at the user-friendly format, I thought that maybe I really could begin to rely on God to guide me through this valley of pain and loss.

From the moment I arrived at the convent, Carla and all the other sisters took me in as one of them, making me feel that I had found a safe place to grieve. I was assigned a room in the guest quarters, a seldom-used part of the convent separate from the sisters' living area. It was very cold there. In the morning I'd enter the bathroom, which had a deep claw tub that was frigid to the touch and no rugs or mats to warm the feet, take off my flannel pajamas, and, remembering to conserve water because many others would need it, do my best to shower using a handheld shower head while crouching in a ball. My whole body would shake, but I didn't feel terribly annoyed. Mostly I felt appreciation, as well as acceptance by the sisters.

Carla tried to do whatever she could to make me feel comfortable. Because it wasn't appropriate for me to eat meals with all the sisters, Carla ate with me so I would not feel alone. She also made me laugh with her habit of leaving plastic spiders out for me to stumble upon. "You just wear that habit as a cover to hide how mean you are," I would tease her, laughing.

Max and Cay invited me to stay with them at our former home in Avezzano on weekends, so I truly had the best of both worlds. Also, because Jonathan and Sheri, along with Wayne, were still living nearby I had real friends to call upon whenever I ventured away from the security of the convent. Everything was in place for me to take steps forward in my grief recovery, although I realized that it was going to be a slow process, as expressed in my journal entry of March 12:

> I felt so normal today. I was surprised by this feeling. The last time I was here, last September, it was more like being on vacation. Today, it just felt like coming home. I also feel a little nervous, but that may be the anticipation of being quiet with myself, something that's been hard for me to do....Today is Bart's birthday. He would have been thirty-nine. I was so looking forward to throwing him his fortieth birthday party! I miss Bart more than words can say. How do I live and find happiness again? I know it will happen. It is just too much to think about. I need to take it slowly.

Soon I plunged into the grief workbook with my full heart and soul. The following are some of my responses to questions posed in the workbook, which I have paraphrased or changed to illustrate the ground I covered doing this grief work:

How would you define your loss?
I had dreams of growing old with Bart, and dreams of watching Benjamin and Samuel grow through the different stages of life to become men who help others in God's love, and are happy and healthy. I wanted to help Sarah through her developmental years and listen to her wonderful laugh.

What is the message that you have especially struggled to hear?
That God is kind and loving. I have needed to understand that he does not

cause accidents but brings the good out in something bad. God is with me in my loss, with love and kindness. He is showing me the way, if only I will listen.

How do you feel toward those you have lost?

Bart, I am so sad you left. You promised me you wouldn't! If we were going to be together in good times and bad times, why did you abandon me when I needed you most? I know you could not have prevented the accident. There are things I think would have changed that day, but it is what it is. I just miss you so much! I need you to hold me!

What else do you still have questions about?

How am I going to live without you, Bart and my boys? You were my life! I don't have one without you guys. What am I going to do? What are my dreams now? How do I fully know if my feelings are correct or if I am faking it? Will I be happy again or lonely forever? How does one not feel alone without your love and your best friend? Can you see me, Bart? What is on the other side of life? I love you, Barton Joel!

How do you define recovery, and what is it going to take for you to recover from this loss?

Recovery is learning to enjoy life again while always remembering my family. It will take many steps, including resolving my anger and confusion toward God. I also need to learn to talk about my feelings more. I believe that being here, around Sister Carla, and using this book will help me make progress. I hope it will bring me understanding instead of confusion and lead me toward having confidence, joy, laughter, and love.

How would you describe true signs of recovery?

Getting up and feeling I can make it through the day.

Taking control of my life.

Living without fear of someone dying or what tomorrow may bring.

Remembering the happy times without the overwhelming feeling of loneliness.

Not being so hard on myself—letting myself do what feels right.

Forgiving the controlling nature of my family and understanding that they will never get it.

Talking about what it is like to lose everyone in your life, in hopes it will help others who are grieving a loss.

Wanting to live and truly start a new life.

Feeling God's presence and having hope for the future.

What do you feel guilty about that may be getting in the way of your recovery?

That I insisted we stop for lunch the day of the accident. That I wouldn't drive afterwards. That I had predicted this would happen but could do nothing to prevent it.

How have you dealt with other losses in your life?

I always had Mom or Dad or Bart to help me. They are the reasons I got stronger and felt smarter. I came to believe I am smart, funny, intuitive, and lovable. They believed in me. Now it is my turn to believe in myself.

What role do you see God playing in your recovery?

To strengthen me and help me find new purpose and a new life. I have forgotten or not been able to ask God for help. It has been too easy to focus on myself and forget to focus on God. If I focus on God and ask him for his help, I know he will make me whole again. I know that Bart, Benjamin, and Samuel are happy being with God. I hope that they can also ask him to help me through this.

What do you need to say to God?

"Dear Lord: I am scared of the journey ahead. You have given me a lot to deal with and I am afraid I won't be able to cope with life. I fear that I will always be sad. So often I find myself overwhelmed and full of anger. I know I need to rely on you, but I can't stop wondering: Will I always have such anger and sadness inside me? Please give me peace from these constant questions and show me what to do."

What do you need to say to others to help yourself stick with your recovery journey?

"Dear Mom: I don't know how I am going to make it without you. You loved me so much and encouraged me in everything I did. You didn't boss or try to control me. Now I need to find my way without you."

"Dear siblings and other family members: It feels too hard to really talk to you now about my grieving. I know you are hurting more than you ever thought possible. Everyone in our family wants me to ask you for help and rely on you, but when we do we get disappointed. I just need to keep letting you know that I need to grieve in the way that's right for me."

What do you still fear?

"Dear Lord: I am having a hard time with my self-esteem. I fear that I will fail in life, in everything. I feel fat, ugly, stupid, and lacking in humor. Please, Lord, give me the self-confidence I need to make it through this. I know I need to feel my feelings more, but mostly I am numb. When I do start to feel my hurt, I usually do something to take my mind off it. I need to listen to how you are directing me, not how to direct myself. I know you want me to have peace, but sometimes I still get angry at you, and I have to learn to give myself permission to tell you when I am angry. I really do feel your presence. There is nothing I can do to make the pain go away. I give it to you, Lord."

About two weeks into my retreat at the convent, March 25 arrived— the first anniversary of the accident. I knew exactly where I wanted to be and with whom I wanted to be: at the orphanage with the children of Sacro Coure to feel the life and love they reflected.

I had already been stopping by there often while staying at the convent, having felt increasingly drawn to one of the children living there, a girl named Diletta. Sister Carla had arranged permission for me to take her shopping, and she came back beaming with pride over her new skirt, sweater, and shoes. On our way to the store, we had passed her dad, who didn't ask who I was or even recognize Diletta at first. Before the accident, when Diletta's birthday had been approaching, Benjamin, Samuel, and I made her a cake to share with her classmates at school, served with Kool-Aid, something none of them had tried. When many of the other kids at the orphanage got to go home to family over the weekends, she never did. This girl, who was the same age as Benjamin, so badly needed to have a real father or mother in her life.

My plan for the first anniversary of the accident was to make choco-late chip cookies with the kids. As far as I knew, these children had never cooked anything. I just couldn't figure out how to explain to a child who didn't speak my language the proper way to crack an egg into the bowl. I imagined six-year-old Erica slamming an egg on the table so hard that it splattered everywhere. I didn't care. I just laughed. Everything about that day was exactly what I needed.

The next day, March 26, the first day of the second year after the ac-cident, I wrote a letter to Bart in my journal, expressing the progress in my grief recovery and what I had learned:

> *Dear Bart: I feel pretty strong right now. I know you have always been proud of me. You have such confidence in me, and it has rubbed off. I am going to make it, with God's help. I have discovered that the loneliness and isolation I have been feeling for so long is a normal part of grieving. As I finally begin to feel more in control, it will make it easier for others to know what I need help with. I need to become much more direct and forthcoming.*

As I continued living in Italy, slowly I began to revisit places I had en-joyed with my family. While these trips triggered memories that could be painful, they also helped me achieve a new sense of exploring such places on my own to take a step forward in my new life. I went back to Orvieto and had a wonderful trip to Rome. I even squeezed in a side trip to Paris with Max and Cay, and Jonathan and Sheri. I appreciated how clean the city was compared to cities in Italy, but the highlight was attending a James Taylor concert. I was entranced listening to his amazing voice, and I appre-ciated his great sense of humor, but what really won my heart was what he did during the second encore. After whispering something to someone on stage, he announced, "I would like to bring out my friend Sting!"

My friends and I had no doubt this was Bart's way of reminding us of the glorious time we all had shared at the Sting concert in Rome so many months earlier. Yes, Bart was still very much with me. I just needed to re-member that it was true.

After I got back to Avezzano, I was granted permission to attend a special meal with all the sisters before going home. Some wondered who I was and why I was there, especially the older nun sitting across from me, who loudly said, "Who is she? Why is she with us? What is going on?" Since she spoke in Italian, I just pretended not to understand. Carla giggled to see that for a change I was nervous while she was in her element, and she was having a good time pouring gobs of the hot sauce that I had brought into her bland soup. But the sisters all turned out to be very sweet. They gave me many lovely gifts: flowers and a bird made of amethyst stone that one of the mother superiors had brought back from Brazil, as well as a beautiful Crucifixion scene on an Abruzzo stone. That summer all the sisters and priests of that region in Italy were scheduled to get together for a conference at which the attendees would each be given the same Crucifixion scene to commemorate the event. Being the only non-nun or priest to be included, I felt like they considered me one of them.

I left for Boise on April 10, nearly a month after I had arrived. As I boarded the plane for home, my mind flashed on an image that seemed to capture what this personal retreat had been about. Before I got to the convent, my state of mind was like opening a door and walking into a room to find papers flying about everywhere, too chaotic to control. Leaving Italy was like opening a door and walking into a room to discover papers neatly tucked in binders, carefully and logically labeled, and securely placed on bookshelves. My life, at last, was finally starting to be put back together.

Chapter 12
Gradual Healing

BACK IN BOISE, IT WAS UP TO ME to decide what to do with the opening for healing that had been given to me by staying four weeks at the convent of Sacro Coure. I certainly can't say that I had seen the light and plowed full steam ahead until I was doing cartwheels and singing songs of joy. I can't outline a clear, concrete path of recovery from grief that I followed every day with confidence, clarity, and conviction. Here's what I can say: I started taking steps in the right direction.

For one thing, after returning from the convent I finally began opening up to Sharon, my faithful counselor who had been listening to me since the first days after the memorial service, now able to trust the help she had been offering me. With Sharon's guidance, I began making and keeping to a schedule for a week at a time after mastering the ability to organize the minutes and hours of each day. One important commitment was my Tuesday lunch dates with my stepfather Dick. I also arranged a grocery delivery system so I would not have to go out in public so often and face pestering questions. I identified the friends I could call upon when I wasn't feeling safe and made a commitment to Sharon, to myself, and to those friends that I would follow through when necessary. That year my new home became my sanctuary. I did my best not to leave its safety unless I absolutely had to. I found that I could have groceries delivered from Albertsons, and practically everything else was available online. This gave me security, if only temporary.

Sharon also taught me the value of screaming now and then. When I was once giving her the rundown of my frustration with the pain I was feeling, all the medication I was taking, and how ugly I felt, she suggested that I let out a scream. It took me a while to find my screaming voice, but when I let loose I noticed that all the frustration that had been bottled up simply dissipated.

After that I was able to scream without prompting. To help clarify how and why this occurred, I first have to explain something I learned about how I was expressing my grief. In those tortuous months right after the accident, when I could barely function and didn't want to go on trying, I would tell myself that I was fully grieving all five of my loved ones who had died. Yet, strangely I could not fully focus on them for very long. Looking back at my suicide attempt, I would say that on the night I took those pills the memory of Bart became much more real, as if I was *really* grieving the loss of my husband.

Then soon after returning from the convent and moving into my new home in Boise I succumbed to another major bout of pain and grief. One memory of this dark time is of grocery shopping in Fred Meyer. I was trying to learn how to eat and cook for one when suddenly I found myself wandering the aisles not knowing who or where I was. Coming around a corner, I looked up to find someone I recognized, my neighbor and Sue's sister-in-law Marlayna, who said, "Jill, are you okay?" As my eyes filled with tears, I replied, "I don't know where I am or what I am doing." "Don't worry," she reassured me, "I'll get you home." Marlayna, who lived just across from me, was another person who got me through a lot that second year after the accident, as she was able to help me lovingly, without judging me.

My new bout of pain and grief also resulted in other frightening incidents that let me know, however, that I was now grieving with greater immediacy and intensity. One night I fell to the bathroom floor, my foot uncontrollably kicked the vent under the sink to the crawlspace below, and I screamed, overcome with the sudden realization that Samuel was dead, too! I had begun to deeply grieve my second loss. I don't know how long I lay there kicking and wailing before I was able to get up and call the one person I could trust to be with me and not judge me for what I was doing: Kelly.

"She was hyperventilating on the floor when I got there," Kelly recalled. "It was like she was having a nervous breakdown. I considered calling an ambulance, which I had thought about doing other nights when she reached out to me in distress, but she seemed to be getting through it, like it was something that had to happen. We both just sat on that bathroom floor, crying together. I stayed until at least midnight, just to be safe."

Without Kelly, I probably wouldn't be alive—not just because she helped me that night of fully grieving Samuel, but because she was *always* there and *always* made me feel loved. I remember on my first Mother's Day after the accident walking into my empty home in Eagle and finding several presents from Kelly, including a letter thanking me for what she had learned from me about being a mom: "relax and enjoy both the innocent and the mischievous; introduce them to all kinds of experiences, even if it's not something you would choose for yourself; do not overprotect but make sure they feel safe; surround them with loving, caring people; let them be free to be themselves and enjoy all that makes them special..."

Now, in this period of rebuilding after my suicide attempt, to further help me she made a commitment: in the middle of her busy life and meeting her own family's needs, she was going to spend every Monday evening with me, giving me something more to count on. Kelly gave me strength and support when almost no one else could, as is evident from her reflections.

Kelly: I don't bond that easily with people. I've always been independent, and I've moved around so much. I never had that one close girlfriend. But with Jill, everything was so different. Before her accident, she had always been so patient with me and had done so many things for me. After her loss, I just wanted to do whatever I could for her. If I could have changed the past for her, I would have done so in a heartbeat.

When I went to visit her in the hospital after her suicide attempt, she was taking a shower. She playfully sprayed water on me, as if to say, "I'm okay now; don't worry." The routine of my coming over to visit every Monday night was my idea, just something to try to get her mind on other things. I would take her to see a movie now and then, but it was surreal how often the plot would lead to a fatal car accident or someone losing their mother or father. I'd also leave her little trinkets to try to lift her spirits: a foosball with eyes; a charm from a bracelet I had when I was little. I would hide them before I left, and she would have to find them.

I'd also visit her on Benjamin and Samuel's birthdays. On Samuel's birthday, we would remember how he used to say he wanted a "reat," which meant "treat," because he loved candy. So we would have candy on his birthday. For Benjamin's birthday, she would want to look at his pictures. I remember one photo of Benjamin riding on his bike. He had not wanted to get off his training wheels and kept riding with the last training wheel on, even though the bike tilted way to one side.

When I would listen to her, there were times I thought it was cruel that she had survived. It just seemed wrong to make a mother survive her husband and children. It affected how I felt and acted with my own kids. I made sure they always wore their helmets on their bikes and used the proper seat belts in the car. When seeing other mothers not doing that, I would be tempted to pull them aside and say, "Let me tell you a story..."

Jill says she wouldn't have gotten through this without me. I would just say I consider her my sister and that she has helped me so much, too. She enabled me to open a part of me that had always been protected. Because of her, I am better in my life as a mother, as a daughter, and as a friend. She gave me a plaque that reads: "To the World You May Be One Person, But to One Person You May Be the World." It still hangs in my bathroom today.

My grief recovery was aided by humor, which happened to be one of Kelly's special gifts. Once she got me to explain to her the little things that used to bother me about Bart, one being that when I'd walk in the room he'd often come up to me and grab my boobs. So Kelly gave me a Boobie Groper so that "when you miss him, you just rub your boobs." Soon after moving into my new home I burned my hand on the broiler and did not even feel it. Laughing hysterically, I called Kelly and said, "Maybe I'll become a cutter since I don't feel any pain." That kind of irreverent humor got me through many a bad day. Sometimes when people ask me the most important ingredient in healing after a loss, I am tempted to say, "Find a Kelly."

Another step in my grief recovery was to somehow learn to love. In this regard, Sharon's useful suggestion encouraging me to get a dog was helpful. She told me this would not only teach me responsibility but maybe how to love something again. Loving had not been easy for me since March 25, 2002, but one summer day in 2003 a friend and I followed directions to a red-roofed house with a litter of puppies. A miniature schnauzer lay next to me calmly, which was his only calm moment during the time I watched him. He was full of spirit and joy—just what I needed to spark my life. I named him Ritter, which means "knight" in German, and took him home. Our conversations were a bit one-sided, but he sure seemed interested. About a month later I showed up in Sharon's office crying. "I love him. And it is *so* scary!" I said, acknowledging the fear of loss that had come up for me while loving another being.

The next assignment Sharon gave me to develop my ability to interact again with people and love was to reconnect more fully with my dad. Before Italy, I had relied on him and he had relied on me. After the accident and his stroke, I felt as if I were letting him down because I was afraid to get close, afraid of losing one more person dear to me. And I didn't have any energy to spare. But now I made a new commitment, reassuring him that I would take care of him if anything further should happen. I also decided that I would do something special for him to show my love and appreciation for him. One day I was lying in my backyard asking God to help me figure out something that would let my dad know how much I loved and respected him. I finally thought of doing something with movies that would celebrate Dad's younger days as well as those of others in his assisted living facility.

The folks at his assisted living facility gave me their old meeting room. I made curtains with big tassels and everything else to create a replica of an old-time cinema, the kind Dad would fondly remember. I bought an old-fashioned popcorn machine and had a projector and screen installed. We asked the residents to write down their favorite movies, and voilà, the theater was ready to show movies. On opening night at the Kraft/Hill Theater, people were lined up around the corner. When I dedicated the theater to Dad in front of everyone, he looked so proud, gazing at me lovingly in a way that reminded me of days past.

I also came to recognize, with Sharon's help, that my drinking was causing pain for the people I loved and that controlling it would help enhance my relationships with others. I stopped for a few months and got myself more together.

I reminded myself often that my main goal was to work on my mental state. For most of the first year after the accident, I had primarily had to deal with my physical state and the fact that the constant pain from my injuries made my emotional pain much worse. I still had physical problems, including sometimes falling with no warning, but now it was time to figure out mentally who this new Jill was. Sharon was there to hold my hand through the search as she explained in a reflection on the time.

> *Sharon*: I earned my doctorate in counseling and specialized in grief and loss. I have worked with many clients who have lost loved ones, so I was very comfortable when I was called on to see Jill. When I first began visiting her in her home, her family's home in Eagle, I could see that she was in great pain. Who in her position would want to live? Some people do something about it, some don't. After her suicide attempt, she learned that she did want to live.
>
> Jill felt like I "got" her. I would tell her that she had to give herself permission to do whatever she needed to do: stare at the wall, cancel plans, etc. She needed to take care of herself first. I never told her she was going to get "better" and that she would have to come to terms with that reality. I said, "You just have to take baby steps." To all my clients in grief I offer my belief in the strength of the human spirit to heal itself, and Jill has a very strong spirit. She would still have days when she wanted to die and be with her boys, but that strong spirit guided her along.

Moving into my new house in Boise was one of the many acts that lifted my spirits. I had chosen a subdivision in southeast Boise, an area of town in which Bart and I had spent much of our time together. My building site was in a cozy neighborhood where I knew I would not feel alone. I brought in many meaningful personal touches. I took a painting of grapes done by one of my neighbors in Italy and had it embedded in the wall above the stove. A neighbor from the Eagle house did all of my cement work, including carefully cutting out the handprints of Benjamin and Samuel from our deck in Eagle. And I asked Peter to make a secret passage to be accessed by a wall that would move when I pulled back on a certain book: *E la camera dei segreti*, the chamber of secrets. This would duplicate a feature we had in our Eagle home we had all liked so much that we would put Christmas lights in there. My backyard area was developed so beautifully by a friend that later my home was included on the Boise home garden tour. For quite a while after I moved in, the garage was so full with things I lacked the energy to sort out that I couldn't even park my car in there. But I didn't care. After selling the Eagle house and claiming this as my home, I felt free.

I even summoned the nerve to become a bit more social again. For starters, I began hosting a wine-tasting at my new house once a month, inviting all my guests to research a particular wine and to bring a homemade appetizer. I also began bringing all the women together for Thanksgiving dinner and for a party on Oscar night, when we dressed up, spruced up the tables, rolled down the red carpet, and interviewed each other as we made our grand entrance. Entertaining had always been a passion of mine, and in these ways Sharon and I discovered how to reintroduce that part of my life.

I also began focusing more on developing my own personal creative expression. I designated one area as my pottery room and put into it the pottery wheel Bart had given me for Valentine's Day. I lost myself for hours in this room, creating pottery. It was such a great escape and so peaceful that I had moments of foreseeing myself as an artist in the future.

The boost in self-esteem I experienced due to decorating my new house was further enhanced when my friend Brian from Micron, whom Bart once worked with, gave me the job of decorating his new home as well. I relished having something else home-related to focus on: paint, new tile, light fixtures, restaining hardwood. I selected a dark stain that matched his cabinets, but while I was out of town he got talked into a lighter color. When he eventually moved out of that house, I laughingly told him it had to have been because of the hardwood stain!

Another important step in my new life was to resolve what to do with my wedding ring. It hadn't felt right to wear it immediately after the accident, but not having it on made me feel guilty. This ring that had felt so right even before finding the man that went with it now felt foreign, not a part of me anymore. I prayed long and hard about what to do, and finally I had the answer. I removed the diamonds and had them placed in the form of a cross. Then I took the few diamonds left over and had them embedded in Bart's band, which I already had been wearing with the band of Benjamin and Samuel's birthstones. Now we were all together again, at least symbolically.

All these changes helped me begin to establish a life as my own person in Boise, instead of just being the wife and mom who lost her boys. I was even noticing room in my heart to possibly love someone new. This opening of my heart began with the idea of exploring the possibility of adopting Diletta, the girl at the orphanage in Sacro Coure I loved so much. I went so far as to have Sister Carla look into what steps would need to be taken. It didn't work out, but I was gratified to learn later that Diletta had found a new home. Adopted by a cousin of Antonella, our Italian friend at Micron, she would at last have the family she so desperately needed.

While I certainly was not ready for an ongoing relationship with a man, I longed for any kind of human touch. It had been difficult to go from a man who could not sleep unless a part of him was touching me to the loneliness that amplified the loss of him. Soon I made a conscious decision to enter into a brief sexual relationship. The touch and closeness I experienced gave me the ability to feel alive again, not only physically but mentally. This man knew my limitations and supported my need to not get emotionally involved—something I would have been against in the past yet now was one more thing that helped me move forward with my new life.

During the months after returning from the convent, I did my best to stay focused on my mental and emotional states, which I regarded as the best way to move forward. This approach included giving myself permission to fully experience my feelings, which was still a major challenge, although I soon discovered a new tool to help. I called it "journaling through music." Music had always carried the capacity to make me feel, and journaling through music had the same kind of therapeutic benefits as writing does for other people dealing with difficult feelings. I would notice how often and easily particular songs would remind me of moments I had shared with Bart, Benjamin, and Samuel, or would bring me to a deeper sense of who they were to me. Since I already had experienced making CDs with Bart in mind, going back to that first silly Christmas present of country music I decided I would put together a CD titled "Life after Bart."

The first song I selected was Joe Jackson's "Stranger Than Fiction" because Bart had played Joe Jackson on our first date. The next song was "Partners" by the Boise band Tauge and Faulkner, a group that had once dedicated this song to Bart and me while we enjoyed a romantic evening at a dinner club. The third song was "Now That I Found You," the Michael Bolton song that had been played for the first dance at our wedding, which I had listened to almost every day after the accident.

I liked the CD so much I decided I would add songs that would focus on the boys, too. The fourth song was "For Rosannah," which is about what you're going to be when you grow up. Next was "One Cool Remove," Benjamin's favorite song for a while. I used to laugh while he would belt out what he thought the lyrics were: "one cool blue moon." Then I chose "One Moment More" by Mindy Smith because it brought me to tears every time she sang the chorus: "Oh please don't go, let me have you just one moment more. Oh, all I need, all I want is just one moment more..." And for the longest time my CD would end with "Personalities" by the local Boise band House of Hoi Polloi, with the lyrics "I just can't wake up. I can't even figure out which way I'm going to look." I related strongly to the feeling of having multiple personalities, almost every day waking up wondering who would be staring back at me.

When I listened to that CD, I would release my emotions of anger, sadness, and happiness. It didn't matter to me that some people who knew me might not easily understand how I related to the songs and why all these feelings were critical for me to feel again and again. It just worked for me. Some days I would sit in my computer room and make a new playlist just for that day. If I was thinking about Samuel, for example, I'd pick a song that described how I felt in the delivery room when I was exhausted because he wasn't sleeping. Or if I was feeling generally depressed I'd choose something appropriate by Depeche Mode or some other group to coax out those emotions. Often I'd delete the list the same day I started it since it had served its purpose.

Sometimes I would play the music while I was doing ceramics. Other times I would just sit and listen—and cry. When I played the music that helped me connect with Bart and the boys, I could actually feel them surrounding me. I didn't always cry, though. Sometimes the music would stir a pleasant memory, and I would giggle. In my day-to-day life, I'd still frequently have moments when I'd experience a feeling and then quickly find something to keep me busy so as not to allow myself to dwell on it. But when I gave myself time to engage in music journaling my feelings came out. And, of course, every time I gave myself that opportunity I had something positive to report back to Sharon.

Sharon also helped me recognize that I needed to come up with new ways to observe holidays and other important occasions in order to establish my own traditions. Christmas had always been a major event for our entire family, but trying to stick with the familiar ritual that first Christmas after the accident just didn't feel right to me. Determined not to repeat that mistake, for Christmas 2003 I did something different. As the holiday approached, my friend Sandy, who was single, told me she was going to celebrate with her parents in Arizona and wondered if I would like to come along. There I played golf in the warm, sunny weather on Christmas Day. I can't say that breaking away from my family routine was easy, but, as Sharon helped me to see, to take care of myself I needed to create a healthy environment for each major occasion from now on.

The second anniversary of the accident in March was approaching quickly, and I knew I would need a good plan to get through that. I wanted to spend it with Kelly. At first we looked into her going back to Italy with me, but when we realized that wasn't going to work we shifted to Plan B: going to Las Vegas. I made this choice partly to go somewhere fun at such a painful time. But I also had another specific goal. I remembered how, when Bart and I had gone to New York together, we had stopped briefly in Tiffany's, where I admired a new cut of diamond soon to be released: the lucida. "That's the most beautiful diamond I've ever seen," I told Bart. Later, we happened to spot the same diamond in Rome, and I had a pretty good idea that Bart had been planning to splurge and get it for me for our tenth anniversary.

Being in Las Vegas would give me an opportunity to make that happen. Kelly and I stayed at the Bellagio, and there was a Tiffany's in the resort. So on the anniversary date, after Kelly and I treated ourselves to a massage and got all dressed up, I bought ½-carat lucida diamond earrings.

Another thing I did to begin my new life was to have a photo taken in Las Vegas of me sitting on a Harley because in the past I had had a desire to become a motorcycle babe. Did I have moments of real laughter during this anniversary trip? You bet. Did I also have moments of crying over all the memories? You better believe it! We even had times when our sick humor emerged through our jokes about The Venetian, but we never actually entered that resort.

This is what life on the grief recovery trail was slowly becoming for me: new bursts of unexpected playfulness, fun, even joy, intermingled with the familiar cloudbursts of pain, sadness, and despair—progress of sorts. One day during this gradual healing I remembered something Bart used to tell me: "Make yourself happy and others will be happy around you." I didn't understand or want to believe what he said then. After all, my happiness had always come from helping other people, starting with Bart and the boys. For years I also had derived joy from knowing I had made a difference in my mom's life and my dad's life, and from helping my friends deal with their life issues. I tried not to consider my own happiness. When I was emotionally drowning soon after the accident, I would occasionally hear echoes of Bart's message but usually ignore them. Now, for the first time, I was finally starting to understand what he had been talking about. "I'm trying, Bart," I imagined saying to acknowledge to him and myself the truth of his advice. From then on, I knew that, despite my grief, I would indeed have to try to make myself happy if I expected to live in an atmosphere where others around me were happy, and if I expected to live a new fulfilling life in the future.

Marrying Bart—
May 8, 1993

My niece Sarah

My mom and her grandbabies Jack, Benjamin, and Samuel

*My dad, Todd, Samuel, Bart, me, and Benjamin
after the US Open—June 2000*

Benjamin, Samuel, and Cinder

Samuel and Benjamin

Samuel, Benjamin, and Sarah at Grandma's house

Samuel, Sarah, and Benjamin the night before we left Boise after my dad's accident

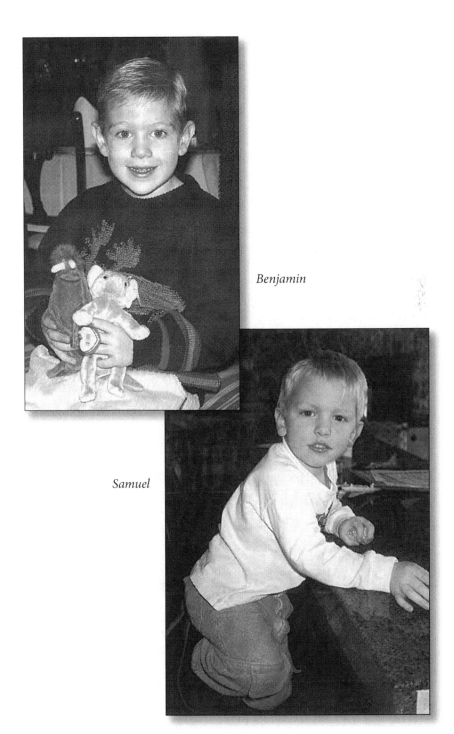

Benjamin

Samuel

Samuel

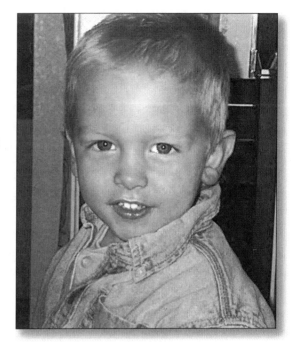

Benjamin, me,
Samuel, and Bart
leaving Capri, Italy

Bart, Benjamin, Samuel, and me in Assisi, Italy

Benjamin posing with ivy

My mom arriving in Rome on the first plane out of the United States after 9/11

Samuel and Benjamin at their favorite castle in Montalcino, Italy

My mom, Benjamin, Samuel, and me at the Colosseum

Benjamin and Samuel dressed for Carnevale, the night before Mardi Gras

Samuel dressed
as a cowboy

Benjamin and Samuel in their tissue hats for Bart's birthday

Samuel and Benjamin thinking the playroom should be their bedroom

Suore Pasquina and her preschool class, with Samuel in center of row 2

*Samuel and
Suore Pasquina*

*Benjamin, Samuel, and
Sarah at Villa d'Este
the day they arrived*

*Sarah and Benjamin
the day before the
accident*

Bart and me the day before the accident

The minivan we were riding in

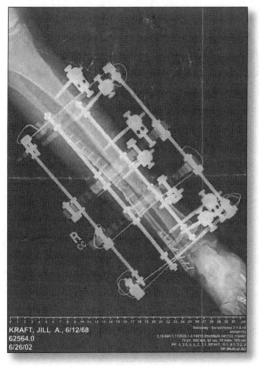

An X-ray of my right leg

The suore and children at the orphanage

Bart's family

Me before Beatrice

Me, Joanna, and Beatrice

Suore Carla and me

Me dressed as a nun

*Sharon,
my grief counselor
and trusted ally*

*Me and Suore Carla
at the Vatican*

My last dinner at the convent, with mother superiors, Suore Carla, and others

John David Thompson

Me and Kelly just before I walk down the aisle to marry John

Marrying John—April 15, 2006

My brother Steve, me, my sister Sue, my dad, and my sister Jody

John and me welcoming Franklin David Thompson

My dad and Franklin

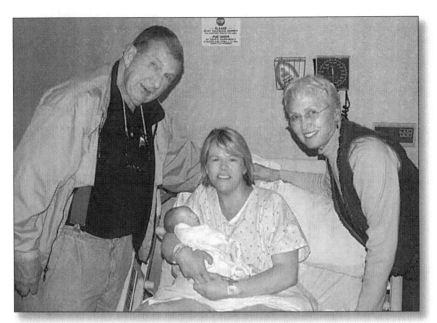

Papa Duane, Franklin, me, and Grandma LaVonne

John and me

Aunt Joni, my dad,
Grandma Gracie, me,
Franklin, and John
at Christmas

Grandma LaVonne
and Franklin

Jace, Franklin, my dad, and James

Franklin's third birthday

*Grandma Gracie
and Franklin*

Jace and Franklin

Franklin and me

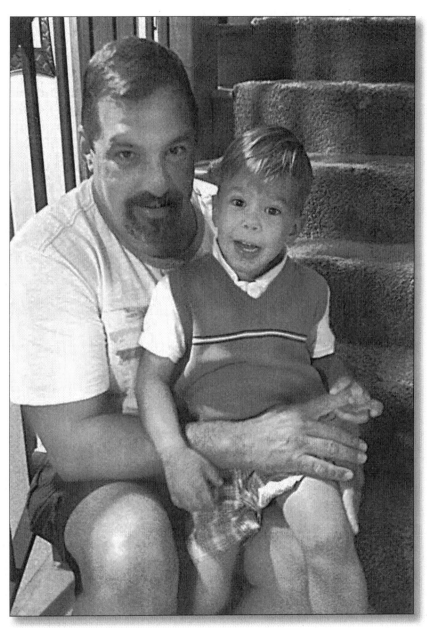

John and Franklin on his first day of preschool

Franklin skiing

Me and Franklin with his mosaic project

Franklin's fourth birthday with friend Drake

John, Franklin, and me in San Diego

Interlude
The Mirror Revisited

AS I LOOK INTO THE MIRROR, *I recognize the reflection somewhat. The woman I see appears older and perhaps a bit harsher, yet there is my hope in her eyes. I am aware that her ceramic pieces reflect talent. There is a natural swing in her golf stroke. Her mother's voice, once speaking words of encouragement, echoes in this empty house, "If you stick with golf, you could make a living from your ability." Looking around I might think I am at a comforting spa, it is so peaceful, so calming.*

But as I glance back at the mirror, I no longer recognize the reflection. What reflects back now is something different, something darker…like a cavern. Where does it lead? What lies deep inside? If I explore it, what if I don't come back? "Keep the rock positioned to cover the entrance," I hear the image whisper.

Now I become aware that the cavern opens to a tunnel that leads to my heart. Oh, I have been there, and know what lurks down the far reaches of that tunnel. I have visited some of the hidden crevices and even faced some of the creatures perched around every corner. It hasn't all been scary and painful but too much of it has, and I fear that one moment of pain surfacing could blast away all pleasant images of life's possibilities. It seems safer to keep the rock positioned over the entrance, keep my eyes focused on external things: creative expression, career, physical acts. If I don't, and I lift my lantern and proceed further and further down the internal underground tunnel where feelings are constantly stirred, I risk opening up my heart, which all too easily could be broken into a thousand pieces that cannot be contained within the framework of the mirror. Yet there are also dreams of something more important, more vital deep inside the tunnel—dreams too dangerous to explore yet possibly the key to revealing a clear image of myself in the mirror. ≈

Chapter 13
The Dawning of Hope

I'VE SEEN THOSE SCENES IN THE MOVIES where a mother, father, son, daughter, or spouse visits the gravesite of a departed loved one. They lay their beautiful flowers. They kneel and touch the carefully polished stone. They talk out loud to the individual at rest there, confiding in them about some problem they need help resolving or expressing their love, often imagining what the deceased is saying to them in response. They convey or receive just the right message, speak a heartfelt thank you, pull themselves together, and get on with the rest of their day.

But this is not my experience at my family's gravesite. I almost never go to the cemetery. I could never have those kinds of intimate grave-side moments with Bart and the boys. It makes their deaths too real and prevents focusing on the wonderful memories of their lives. As soon as I confront the realities of the accident—the screeching brakes, the melting metal, the stench of their blood—I want to run away. If I stay with that scene, I risk going back to the time I was on the fence between insanity and reality. So if I visit the gravesites of Bart, the boys, and Mom I can't wait to get back in my car and go shopping or retreat to my safe home.

At my family's plot, there is Mom's plaque with a rainbow on the back; my words for Bart: "The light of my life, I love you tons—Jill"; and the passage I selected for the boys: "Even though I walk through the valley of the shadows of death I will fear no evil, for you are with me. I love you, my dar-ling little angel boys." I cringe when I read *darling*, which was not supposed to be in there. Every night I would say to them in their bed: "I love you, my little angel boys!" There's a photo of Samuel in his cowboy hat; another of Benjamin with a rainbow below his name; one of the two boys with their arms around each other; and one of Bart on the ferry near Seattle.

On the rare occasions when I have visited the cemetery in recent years, I have noted some amazing coincidences that have made me consider the larger context of my tragedy. According to information on grave markers and in newspapers, a high school classmate of mine in Weiser lost a child in 2002, the same year as my accident. Then, a few years later, three more of his children died in another accident when they were going to school in a car driven by a friend on an icy road. Their graves are only yards away from the graves of my family. I wrote the classmate a letter of condolence: "My loss is different from yours. I can't understand what you're going through; no one can. But perhaps I can be a good listener." However, I never mailed the letter, unsure about whether it would help or hurt.

Yet due to this and other experiences during the first few years after the accident, I came to better understand that other people, including those close me, had suffered and would suffer. I remember at one point early on feeling as though no one else I cared for would ever hurt in such a traumatic way. And I definitely believed I had suffered enough to live the rest of my days without additional trauma. But over time I realized that this perspective was naïve, that there are no rules about the occurrences of trauma in people's lives.

I also discovered from my experience with grief recovery during the first years following my loss, that it doesn't necessarily get easier. Yes, I took some significant steps to focus on my healing and regain a measure of control in my day-to-day life after the wake-up call of my suicide attempt. Yes, I did find more appropriate means of feeling my pain, sorrow, and fear. Yes, my pottery making and other creative endeavors were positive new activities that helped me deal with grief. Yes, I made a stronger commitment to call upon my most trusted allies if I started sinking into a dark abyss again. But did the intense struggle end? No. In fact, sometimes I wondered if it wasn't actually worse.

I wasn't faithfully keeping a journal in the period from one to three years after the accident. But when I did reflect on my inner thoughts, what I usually wrote was something like the following:

Lord,

Help me understand why I am surrounded by death. Life is difficult for everyone, but it truly feels as if I am in a funnel spiraling down again. Can't I be who I was? I know they are not coming back, but I am still lost without them. I wander around daily wondering what the hell I am supposed to do. I try to walk through yet another day when I still have no idea how a mother fills a day without her children. There were times, before the accident, when I would look forward to having a day when I would no longer have to take care of anyone but myself. I appreciated those opportunities to go off to a movie, take a quiet coffee break, or go to lunch with a friend. Every parent needs that from time to time. But that was a few hours of reenergizing myself. Now all of this empty time is depleting my energy.

I want to wake up to my boys' laughter. To their hugs, kisses, and, yes, even their knee in my back from crawling into bed with me. To know exactly what the day has in store. As a mom, my goal each day was to love unconditionally, and to teach, learn, and laugh. I was a great mom. Now I am just a poor, misguided, sad blob that takes up air and space. I want to be happy again—to contribute to this world until I am laid to rest with my family. Do I still dream of being with them? Would you blame me if I did, Lord?

As I look back on those years of slow adjustment, I see an image of myself hovering, watching over my life, existing in the flesh but disconnected from myself and other people, unable to fully engage in my current life because of fear that sorrow would take over.

Often when I tried to connect with other people around me, I would wind up lashing out at them in anger not really meant for them but anger that had nowhere else to go. For example, one St. Patrick's Day night when I went out with a group of friends from college and some other folks, while drinking and talking my intense feelings got stirred. I reached for an extra drink or two to try to numb them. The next thing I knew, something was said to me that I blew all out of proportion, and I replied with a hurtful comment. This type of scenario played out many more times than I care to admit, though I can't remember all the details because when you add a little alcohol to a steaming cauldron of grief you serve up one explosive, memory-clogging cocktail.

Attempts to connect with family members also often resulted in miscommunication. Looking back, I can see, for instance, that I had expected my sister Sue to take charge after the accident and be like a mother figure to me when she didn't have the ability to do so—an unrealistic expectation. *I* had to change instead of anticipating that *she* should change.

Due to lack of communication, I lost many friends during the first two or three years after the accident. I was never sure if it was my grief or their grief blocking meaningful interaction, but somehow we just couldn't get through to one another. And the longer I'd go without contact with someone I used to know well, the harder it was for me to pick up the phone and reach out to them. I would imagine such a conversation beginning with my sharing the small, simple tasks I had undertaken that day, which I would report only to fulfill their expectation that things were going a little better for me. But even if I was having a good day, I knew I would be tempted to add some lament about how life was continuing but my family was not, and then they'd probably say something about God having some plan, and I'd shout, "God isn't our puppeteer! He doesn't create accidents. He doesn't spare some people and not others. Shit happens. Sometimes there are just no answers." So since I didn't want to have such a dialogue I wouldn't pick up the phone at all.

Still, I was constantly on the lookout for any possible answers to my own nagging questions or any kind of reassuring signs. A few years after the accident, I said a prayer to sleep through the night, which was still a relatively rare experience. I wound up having what began as a nightmare of being with Samuel when a tsunami hit. I was holding on to him for dear life when I awoke with a start, quickly realizing that in the dream I had survived but had had to let Samuel go. I didn't want to fall back to sleep for fear of facing the void that would come next, reminding me of my reality, but I did nod off. Surprisingly, the dream took a different direction. I came across my little guy innocently watching cartoons. "Samuel, how did you make it through the tsunami?" I asked. "I was holding my breath under the water, and I found one of those asthma things (inhaler). Every time I needed air, I just used that," he calmly explained. I got to hold him for the rest of the dream. That was one dream I looked forward to sharing with Sharon and Kelly. In the end, though, it was just a dream.

In a way, my whole life those days was a slow process of waking up from the big dream of being with Bart and the boys again. As alluring as it was, it wasn't real, and I had to fully accept the loss of them and figure out how to get through life without them. Maybe, though, I thought I could at least be with them in some middle-of-the-night dreams like the second part of that one with Samuel when I could hold them again, if only for a moment and not in the flesh.

On rare occasions, I had the comforting experience of feeling their presence in a waking state. One summer evening I was in my kitchen preparing to attend Boise's Shakespearean festival. While washing grapes to take with me, feeling typically blue I said silently to Bart, "I'm so sad, I wonder if you would even love me?" Suddenly the music playing softly in the background boomed so loud I feared it would blow every speaker in the house. Since my dog Ritter was in the music room, I assumed he must have hit the volume control. But as I ran toward the controls, the cabinet was closed and Ritter, just waking up on the couch, looked up questioningly. As I opened the cabinet, the volume knob went up loud, then soft, then loud. I screamed, "Just stop!" The knob slowly moved to the correct position. Walking back to the kitchen, I had a feeling I should listen to the words and heard: "I will always love you. You will be mine forever...." Convinced that Bart had just sent me a message, I eagerly headed off to the festival in a much better mood.

I dreaded the birthdays of Bart and the boys, though I'd do my best to honor their memory on such days. Since Bart liked scotch I would have a sip of scotch on his birthday in March. On Benjamin's birthday in June, I would make a point of cooking *pasta con burro* (pasta with butter) because that had been his favorite dish for a while. For Samuel's birthday in September, candy and horses were the connecting themes. I often asked Kelly to come over to help me get through those days. Sometimes I would take out the old family photos and home videos, but after a few minutes I would have to stop looking at them. On many days around their birthdays, I never even got out of bed.

Also, it was still painful to be around someone I was just getting to know because I was aware that the conversation would inevitably shift to the subject of husband and children. When I was invited to go to the Bahamas to attend the wedding of my friends Jim and Zeke, the inspiration for naming my leg contraption Beatrice, I decided to make the trip. I wanted to be there, not because they needed me but to prove to myself I was capable of doing things on my own. Supporting them in their commitment of love gave me strength and opened my heart yet a little more.

While attending the big event, I stayed in a lovely resort they had chosen, with an assigned roommate I had never met. When this woman immediately told me all about her happy life with her husband and kids, I quickly spilled out the morbid details of my story, punctuating it with the admission that "some days I just want to die." She freaked out, no doubt afraid that I was going to kill myself that night right in front of her! So I had to reassure her that she would be spared a wedding suicide, that I had passed that threshold of trying to kill myself, that what I had said just reflected a feeling.

As the third anniversary of the accident drew near in March 2005, I decided that the best way to get through it would be to go back to Italy. I asked a college friend, Jody, to spend two weeks there with me. As I prepared for the trip, I was excited to show Jody my favorite places but anxious about the memories that would come flooding back. Surprisingly, I held up well. It was a special delight to see Sister Carla and the other sisters at Sacro Coure. We stayed a couple of nights in Positano, where I told Jody I had some unfinished business. I easily found my way back to the roof-top art studio that had captured Bart's attention almost four years earlier. It was time, finally, to honor the promise I had made back then to buy a painting by the artist he had selected. As I looked around, I said aloud, "Okay, Bart, which one do you choose?" My eyes went directly to a painting titled *Positano*. Which perfectly captured the beauty of our favorite spot in Italy on the Amalfi Coast, by far the most magical, beautiful place I'd ever experienced. I took that painting home and still have it today. Every time I pass it at the bottom of my stairs, I feel the warmth of my family and the happiness we experienced in Italy.

Jody and I then headed north to another favorite town, Montalcino. We stayed at a hotel where the people recognized me. This threw me for a bit of a loop, and I covered my tears with wine. The next day, as I tried to escape the embarrassment of my previous night's drunkenness, I backed our rental car into a ditch. We could not stop laughing! On our way to Abruzzo for our final good-byes, we decided we would head to Rome in hopes of attending the viewing of Pope John Paul II, who had died during our stay in Montalcino. After standing in line for at least two hours and not moving an inch, we realized there was more to be done in this grand city before departing while I held the memory of his passing in my own way.

"What an amazing man!" I wrote in my journal. "If I could do only a quarter of what Pope John Paul has done for God…I feel so inadequate in God's eyes. I don't want to disappoint him or disappoint any of my family who have passed on, but too often I don't have the energy for anything. Lord, give me strength, peace, and love. Amen."

Coming home, I began to feel a welcome shift in my mental state toward a more positive outlook. Once again, Italy had calmed me, given me hope. A journal entry written just after returning to Boise reflects my new outlook:

I love and miss my family so much, but it's time to move into the new person I have been slowly becoming. Someday I will find that person inside me who loves, laughs, and hopes with anticipation for each upcoming day. I miss her! I will honor their memory by living my life. I can find the way to enjoy my current life while I also remember.

I was grateful to be having hopeful feelings about my own future. Yet, even more surprising, I began to believe that I could love again. I wrote in my journal that April:

Dear Lord,

I believe I am ready to share my life again. I know when given an opportunity I will be able to love again, probably even better than before. Who knows when that will happen or how, but it will. I would much rather share my life with someone, and I know I am ready. How to meet someone, and whether or not they have the strength to love me, is a different story. This person will need to be confident enough to handle my love for Bart. Strong enough to support me through the sorrow I will face in the days and years ahead. And loving enough to understand. I give this all to you. Amen.

Now I believed that I had accomplished sufficient grief recovery and had a heart open enough to make someone else a part of my new life.

Chapter 14
The Heart That
Learned to Open Again

By now I was doing my best to get out of the house and socialize at times, hoping I could interact with new people without disappearing into my past. My plans for the evening of April 27, 2005, were simple: a friend and I would head over to "Alive After Five," Boise's spring and summer outdoor music, dancing, and fun event. We'd listen to a little music, have a few drinks, hopefully laugh a little, and maybe even flirt a bit if the opportunity arose—just a pleasant evening out of the house, away from sad thoughts.

But when the weather turned stormy and Alive After Five got canceled, we needed a Plan B. I remembered that my niece had recently begun bartending at the Red Feather and suggested we go there for dinner. My friend and I were sitting at the bar chatting when the door flew open and a most handsome man walked in out of the storm. As he sat down next to my friend, we made eye contact. I figured that would be the extent of our communication because my friend was thin, cute, and carrying very little noticeable life baggage. In contrast, I was about sixty pounds heavier than before the accident and exceeded my limit on baggage! Strangely enough, he chose to talk to me.

In those days, after having had my fill of telling strangers about the accident and then having to deal with their reaction, I was trying to follow the "three strikes and you're out rule." Ask me once if I have children, and I divert the question: strike one. Ask me again, and I divert more strongly: strike two. And you don't want to see what happens if you ask me a third time.

This handsome man, whose name was John, asked twice in the usual sort of way. As he started to speak again, my niece was standing behind me facing him and drawing her index finger across her throat in the "kill it" sign. But this guy ignored the sign and blabbered something about a husband and kids. I took a deep breath. *He asked for it*, I thought. *I'm going to lay it on him.*

"Well, three years ago I was living with my husband and two boys in Italy," I began, and I could tell he was listening closely but with no clue of what was coming next. "My mom, sister, and niece came to visit. On our way from Venice to Florence a semi truck lost control and hit us head-on, killing everyone except my sister and me."

And in the ensuing split second that followed I prepared myself for the shocked response, the inappropriate questions, the need to reassure him, the pain in my gut. But instead he had an immediate and natural answer.

"That sucks!" he said. What better response could there be? I just exhaled once and started laughing.

"It sure does," I said as I continued chuckling.

Then we just continued on with our conversation. Sure we talked more about what happened to me, but we discussed many other topics, too. I thought: *This is a guy I could really imagine getting to know. Of course, he'd have to want to get to know me, too. And even if he could respond so perfectly to hearing about what happened, he still knows I've got this baggage.*

When I got up to leave, John asked for my phone number. I gave it to him, but I figured that if he did call it would only be out of pity so I would need to be ready to create a way out for him. He had told me he lived in Spokane and was only in Boise for work. This was Wednesday, and he was leaving early Friday for a rafting trip. When he called the next morning, I made up some excuse why I couldn't meet for coffee that day. I expected him to just gracefully exit stage left or make some vague promise to call me next time he was in town.

But instead he asked, "Well, what do you have going on tomorrow?" Another surprise.

"What about your rafting trip?" I inquired.

"Oh, I can just leave a little later," he insisted.

So we had coffee that Friday morning. By the time he got up to leave for his trip, four and a half hours had gone by. And when he was about two hours outside of Boise he called me again to ask if he could phone me periodically after he got back to Spokane. For the next month, John and I talked on the phone almost every day. As I wrote in my journal, this experience was already changing my outlook:

> John called again first thing this morning. He is such a nice guy, and talking to him makes me feel good, even though I think I do a bit too much sharing. I am especially excited because I will be able to see him again next week! Maybe it is just a friendship, or maybe it will turn into more. No worries, because I am having fun. Fun with him, fun with my friends, fun with my life. Thank you, God, for allowing me some kind of happiness. Help it to continue. In Jesus's name, Amen.

Around this time, my family was getting together for a very important event. Jody and Paul had established the SCARF Foundation in memory of my niece Sarah. It supports young new mothers in learning the importance of reading to their children, starting at the beginning of their lives. Sarah loved to read. I still have her first book entitled "Aunt Jill!" In previous years of the event, I did not want to detract from this celebration of Sarah by participating with my ongoing grief, plus I felt that the strain in relating to my family since the accident did not help my healing. But this year I wanted to be there for Jody and Paul. I knew it would be difficult to attend on my own so I invited John to come for support, and he agreed.

We met first in McCall, where we enjoyed our second date. Later, he accompanied me to the bike hike for Sarah. Then John and I were together a week before we had to say good-bye, except it wasn't a real good-bye at all. My journal entry for May 28, 2005 reads:

> It is one week since John and I got together again, and I am in love. Scared, yes! It seems like we were together much longer than a week. The first night in McCall was wonderful. We couldn't stop talking....I know a lot could happen, but I do feel he is my lifelong partner. I have never met a sweeter

man. He makes me feel safe, comfortable, sexy, and nice. I am so happy! He has held me when I have cried, and I held him when he thought his dog was dying. He also makes me laugh and be silly…God, I give us to you. Forgive me if I have moved too fast. Help us not to hurt one another. Guide us in the direction you want us to go. Thank you for John coming into my life. Thank you for helping me become ready for him. Be with me in continuing my grieving. Help me to be honest with him and myself. Give John the strength to deal with Bart and the whole situation. I know John doesn't understand you, but deep down he believes. Give him comfort. I love you, Lord. In Jesus's name, Amen.

Finding the will to love again did not make my grief dissolve. It was still very much a part of who I was and how I would be in this new relationship, wherever it would take me. In one way or another, the past would influence almost everything that happened to me and to us.

My relationship with John continued moving quickly. John confided that he was a big snowmobiler and had always wanted to live in the Mc-Call area, a beautiful region of mountains and rivers north of Boise. So he sold his house in Spokane, and I helped him find a place in Cascade, a straight shot up Route 55 from Boise. This was his dream home. And for a city chick I knew it would make a nice cozy cabin, perfect for our regular romantic get-togethers.

One weekend while visiting John in Cascade I had to leave for Boise earlier than anticipated. I had brought my dog Ritter to John's house with me, and since I would be coming back there after just one night at home I decided to leave Ritter with John. When I called John that night, he told me that Ritter was missing. That news was alarming since my cat Jazzy had disappeared from his home the night before. The day after Ritter disappeared, we spotted a two-foot owl casing the property. I never saw Ritter again. Now I had experienced yet another loss, the death of the first being I had opened my heart to after the accident. I felt pain, but with John's support I was able to move forward.

During our first year of dating, John and I went to see Sharon together for couples counseling. "Jill, you need to learn how to bring John into your life, baggage and all," she said. "John, you need to bring Bart and the boys into your life, too, and have a relationship with them. You need to understand that there will be days when Jill will not get out of bed, and it will not be helpful to her if you are too pushy about what you think she needs to do. You cannot judge her behavior the same way you might judge someone who has not experienced this many losses. Bart, Benjamin, and Samuel are a part of Jill, and they will always be a part of what the two of you have together. This is not something that a person can get over."

John nodded. He had already seen plenty of evidence of the boys being part of me. There were days when I felt so sad I couldn't get out of bed. John never forced me, but at times he encouraged me to make it to the front door, then a little ways up the hill, then to the end of the long driveway to the mailbox, enough exercising to often change my mood. And when I needed to cry, John would hold me—at least for a while, until he would try to get me moving again. I was more and more amazed at how anyone could allow me to openly grieve instead of trying to cover it up. Even when I was turning into that old familiar oozing, gaping wound, he still loved me, while others probably would have run. Something had been stirred in him, too, as he expressed it:

John: When I met Jill that first night and she told me her story, I was hearing echoes of dark spots in my own life. And I told Jill some of it during our first date. In October 2001, I had been in a car accident near Pullman, Washington. It was 7:30 am, and I was driving a Dodge Diesel pickup on my way to Boise to make a sales call. The car in front of me on the two-lane highway was going slower than me, and I pulled out to pass him. I was going about 70 miles an hour. A car pulled out of a cross street on my left and turned right, without stopping at the stop sign. I thought I could avoid the head-on collision by going into the ditch—he did, too. I hit his Honda Accord on the driver's side door. I smashed my knee against the dash and tore ligaments in my lower back, but the air bags came out and I was saved. I hurried out of my pickup, rushed to the Accord, shut off the ignition, and called 911…The coroner said the driver died instantly and didn't suffer.

The car ahead of him at that cross street had turned the other way, and that driver saw it all happen in the rearview mirror. It was his girlfriend! "It's not your fault," she told me at the scene. "He was in a hurry to go elk hunting and..." When I learned this deceased driver was a veterinarian student, I thought he must have been a good guy because the vets I knew were good people. A chaplain came to the accident scene and asked me if I wanted to talk. "No, I'm fine," I said. But I couldn't sleep that night, just kept thinking of that Metallica song "One," in which the guy loses his ability to speak and see. That song was playing when I had rushed to his car and felt for a pulse.

I was married at the time, and when my father-in-law came to the scene and hugged me I broke down. My doctor sent me to a counselor, who gave me tools to help right away. When I told her it was just a wrongful death, she said, "Tell me a rightful death." She taught me a visualization exercise to relax me, asking me to think of being at a warm, sandy beach. I actually thought of something that fit better for me: a meadow with three feet of fluffy snow. It was a quiet and peaceful scene, and thinking of it helped me sleep. She also told me to write a letter to the victim's family but not send it. So I wrote to his parents, telling them how I really wanted to know who their son was and how sorry I was.

This wasn't the first time I was given tools for recognizing grief and dealing with it. In the 1990s I lost five friends to various accidents: a fishing boat accident, an accident while hitchhiking, and a car accident. After my close friend Brian died, I saw a counselor and got the book *Good Grief* by Granger E. Westberg. Following a suggestion in that book, I went to Puget Sound, put my hands in the water, and said good-bye to all my friends who had died.

Life is a toolbox—you get a pipe wrench, and you never know when you might use it. I was carrying those tools about grief when I met Jill. When she informed me about her accident, I thought I'd like to get to know more about this person, thinking maybe there was something I could do to help. I would hold her hand and try to give her a little nudge sometimes, but the truth is that being with Jill was also helping me right from the start. For one thing, she's brought me out more. She tends to be the social one, and I'm pretty private when it comes to my feelings. I learned from the unconditional love she showed her friends. And I learned from the pride she carried for her boys. One day I said to myself, "Wow, how did you get selected to meet someone so strong?" My family was not warm and fuzzy. I was learning what it really meant to love someone in your life every day.

While John was learning what it took to love someone close for the first time, I had to relearn it. When it would get hard for me, I would gain strength from knowing that I would never let go of my love for Bart. Many people who knew me couldn't understand that because I had someone new. No one would ever ask you to stop loving your children, so why your husband? The truth was that although Bart had died, my love had not. Fortunately, this was something John seemed to understand.

> *John*: Who am I to say she can't be in love with her husband who passed away? It's one of those things I just have to accept. Mostly it seems like she is reminiscing about her "first life." She's kind of died and come back—not died with them but with her heart still grieving. It's sort of like she's a canvas of a famous artist, like Michelangelo, whose work was never finished in his eyes.
>
> Sometimes I try to bring humor into the situation. I believe that sometimes you've got to look at serious things in life a bit lightly. Once I was out with Jill wearing a T-shirt with the words *Dead Guy Ale* on it. I just wasn't thinking when I put that on. But then the name just started popping up. When I ordered a Sierra Nevada beer once, a bartender brought Dead Guy Ale by mistake. Another time in Alaska we were at a liquor store ordering stuff for a boat trip, and when we went to launch the boat a six-pack of Dead Guy Ale fell out. Neither of us had ordered it. When these coincidental things would happen, Jill and I would both laugh. "If Bart saw this, he would crack up, too," we'd say. Then we would have a drink and toast Bart.

While John was learning not be jealous of Bart, I had to master the ability to trust again. After all, I had trusted Bart when he had said everything would be okay in Italy. I had trusted my brother and sisters after the accident when they had claimed they would take care of me. I had trusted many of my friends when they had stated they would stand by me. I had trusted people all my life, putting their feelings ahead of my own. Now I had to learn to trust other people while also paying attention to my own feelings and intuitions about situations. "Please, Lord, show me strength and peace in love," I wrote in my journal. "Show me how to be a friend and lover. Help John and me connect deeply with each other and you."

John and I were getting closer every day. One morning I was handling a money transaction in town when I caught myself almost saying, "My husband will take care of that," meaning John, not Bart. Yet when I would see anything that reminded me of Bart I would still sometimes long for the past. We had had such a good life together, and I still loved him so very much. I could also still hear all of them in my mind. But now their voices did not trouble me so much since I understood that they would be a part of me forever. Knowing that John was able and willing to accept them in his life was such a gift.

On the chilly night of February 21, 2006, I was upstairs praying to God, wondering if I was forcing my relationship with John or if this was really what God wanted. I prayed, "Lord, please make it obvious. We all know I have a head injury!" Immediately after I had finished this prayer John yelled, "Hey, Jill, will you join me in the hot tub?" As we gazed up at the stars while warming in the hot tub, he asked, "Will you be my wife?" I said yes without hesitation.

We began planning our wedding for April 15. We went to a lodge in Washington, taking Kelly and John's friend Eric as witnesses. Kelly walked me down the aisle to the Santana song "Love of My Life " as Susan Cornwell, who had participated in my first wedding ceremony, sang. It was a beautiful, private ceremony, just what I needed. John and I wrote our vows:

John, I'm so grateful for the way you love me...without judgment or condition...with sincerity and the quiet reassurance that feels so comfortable, so right. You show me in so many ways how much you care for me...by your sensitivity, your honesty, and your willingness to face whatever challenges come our way. John, your love helps me to know that I'm a lovable person. And though I never thought I would need anyone as much as I need you you've taught me that relying on someone doesn't have to mean giving up my own strength and independence...but that together we are stronger than either one of us could be alone. John, thank you for your wisdom, your gentle support. But, most importantly, thank you for your love! Love forever, Jill.

Jill, I love you so much that I want to protect you from harm.... To be there for you whenever you need me. I want to make your life more beautiful than anyone else ever has. I want to be the one who makes you smile when you wake with the dawn.... To be the song in your heart, and on your lips when you close your eyes at night. I want our togetherness to grow and to last. Beyond today, beyond tomorrow, beyond forever. Jill, you are the one love who has moved my heart to soar on the heights.... You are the love of my life! All my love, John.

John created our rings, with everyone's birthstones scattered on them—Benjamin's, Samuel's, Bart's, John's, and mine. Thus we became united as one family both symbolically and emotionally.

We had planned to honeymoon in St. Lucia, but I forgot my passport, prompting a quick change in itinerary. After calling the resort we were to visit as part of Plan A, we found that we could postpone our stay until a later date at no extra charge, so my mistake resulted in two honeymoons. Plan B was to go to Key West, where John convinced me to go snorkeling. Whenever I would go snorkeling, I would hear the song from the movie *Jaws* running through my head. I held on to John's arm for dear life. Coincidentally, when he later he took me deep sea fishing, I caught a twelve-foot shark.

When John told me he wanted to live full time in Cascade because he loved being so close to nature, where he could go river rafting and snow-mobiling regularly, I agreed to remodel his dream house into a place we both could call home. My Boise home was far too important to my ongoing healing to sell, so I was pleased when John's mom, Gracie, moved into it. This not only brought her closer to her son but gave me a place to escape to when nature became too quiet.

My new path was set. I would still often get scared. I was still regularly grieving. But my life, which I had for so long believed was never going to move forward even an inch, had, in a very short time, chugged many miles down the highway.

Chapter 15
The News: It's a Boy!

JOHN AND I WERE IN NEW YORK CITY heading off on our second honeymoon when one night at dinner I noticed him peering over at a table next to us, where a couple and their two children were seated. He put his wine glass down, looked directly at me, and said, "I think we should try to have a family."

"Really?" I asked. This was a surprise. Soon after we had been married, John had let me know he didn't think he wanted children. I told him that was okay because I was scared to feel love for a child again. Now something had shifted for John.

"You've told me so many stories about being with Benjamin and Samuel. You're just such a wonderful mom," he explained. "I know I have a lot to learn to be able to love like that, but with you I think I can do it. Let's bring a child into our lives."

So we kept talking. And I did some soul-searching—was I still too frightened to feel that kind of love for a new child, to be a mother to someone other than Benjamin or Samuel, to risk being vulnerable to what life could hand out? Or was I prepared to add to the union that John and I had created and open myself to all the joy and sadness that could come?

"I'm ready. Let's start a family," I said finally, suddenly feeling excited with new expectations.

I discovered that I was pregnant on June 2—Benjamin's birthday. Could there be any other more positive sign? I wondered. John and I started mapping out all the changes the birth of a child would bring. Certainly everything would go all right, I convinced myself.

Then on June 12, my birthday, I had a miscarriage. Instantly I felt my heart shatter. But instead of being knocked down by a tidal wave of grief and loss and staying submerged for months, I got up and began applying the lessons I had learned about grieving with John's support. I did lots of writing about my feelings, including reliving the details of my first miscarriage before Benjamin had come along. I had had that miscarriage the same night I learned that my dad had suffered his first stroke. With my focus on Dad at the time, I never got to grieve the loss of that child, especially because I soon got pregnant with Benjamin. So I recognized that I needed to grieve for that first loss as part of my grieving for losing this child with John.

Then, much sooner than I ever could have imagined, I got a big surprise. John and I were traveling to my brother's home for Thanksgiving that year when I got off the plane and had to go to the bathroom. That is when I noticed the bleeding indicating that I was pregnant again! We called our doctor immediately, and he told me to relax and put my feet up. Though I tried as best I could, I was convinced I was going to lose this child, too. I ended up spotting throughout the pregnancy, prolonging my fear about losing the baby. But this child had other ideas.

As I prepared for an ultrasound, I was convinced the baby was a girl. That would be fine, I felt; I was ready for a whole new experience of mothering and with a daughter I wouldn't be so readily reminded of the vivid memories of two boys running around the house.

But the technician reported, "It's a boy!" She probably wondered why I reacted with tears. I was having another boy? How strong did God think I was?

By this time in my grief recovery, though, I was able to allow myself to fully experience my feelings, as reflected in a journal entry from December 2007, just past the halfway point of the pregnancy:

> John and I have grown together so much, which is a good thing seeing that we are going to have a baby boy in a few months! His name will be Franklin David Thompson. I am so excited, scared, happy, sad. Excited I will have a little guy. Scared something will happen. Happy to have a chance to love so deeply again. Sad because Benjamin and Samuel and Franklin won't know each other. Preparing for this new little boy makes Benjamin and

Samuel's deaths very real right now. I miss them both so much! And what if I can't be as good a mom with Franklin as I was with them?

My anxiety about the upcoming birth didn't disappear, but my excitement was definitely building. Not wanting to let anything else get in the way of my enthusiasm, I recognized one other concern that I had to address. In the hospital, many nurses, fellow mothers, and their families, and other stuff or visitors would be coming up to me to share in our celebration and take a peek at our new arrival, which would mean hearing the standard question, "Is he your firstborn?"

Then I'd feel obligated to explain: "Well, not exactly. You see, six years ago I was living in Italy with…" Or some people in the hospital who had heard about the accident from the local media coverage at the time might ask me how I was doing or volunteer comments about how far I had come. I knew that any explanations of my past life would undermine the positive experience I wanted John and me to have in connection with the birth of our child.

Fortunately, Sharon had an excellent suggestion for how to avoid this kind of unwelcome discussion. "Post a note on your hospital room door," she advised. "Explain the story to everyone enough so they will get it. Then tell them what you need from them when they come up and talk to you."

Consequently, I wrote a simple note about what had happened in Italy, saying that if people really wanted me to explain more, I might choose to share some happy memories about my boys myself but needed to do this without feeling obligated to talk about the accident. For too long it had almost felt as if I had lost the right to talk about Bart and the boys because people wouldn't know how to react and then there would be tension. Now I was trying to direct how people would relate to me and my past so I could stay focused on the joy of giving birth. This strategy worked. I avoided complicating, or even spoiling, this special experience by having to deal with other people's reactions to hearing news they couldn't possibly know how to handle.

On April 14, 2008, Franklin David Thompson was born. He weighed six pounds, ten ounces, and from the first moment I loved him so much! He was adorable, even when he cried. In my first journal entry as a mother to this beautiful boy, I wrote:

Dear Lord,
Thank you so much for Franklin! Please give me the knowledge to raise him in an honest, happy, loving environment.

Once that first wave of motherly bliss began to wear off, I started to express the full range of my feelings in my journal:

I am tired and definitely have many emotions swarming around in me. I feel so happy when I just look at Franklin, and I also miss Benjamin and Samuel so much. Franklin has brought all the wonderful memories back: how they talked, how they felt, how they smelled. Creating new memories with Franklin is wonderful, but sometimes it just feels like Benjamin and Samuel should be with us, too. And already I am wondering: how do I teach Franklin about his brothers without scaring him or making him sad, too?

In addition to feelings of sadness about Benjamin and Samuel, I continued to fear that something could also happen to Franklin. It was not a fear that threatened to paralyze me every day, but it would sometimes surface and affect me when I least wanted it to. For example, my friend Jody invited me to her wedding on May 3, just a few weeks after Franklin's birth. She had moved to Washington with her husband, and the wedding was to be held outside Portland. Jody was the friend who had graciously accompanied me to Italy for the third anniversary of the accident, and with whom I had stayed after my suicide attempt before going to the convent at Sacro Coure. Jody used to join me for relaxing excursions floating down the Boise River on a raft, and she was a regular at women's social gatherings in my new home in Boise. For a while, she had been the only person other than Kelly whom I really trusted. There was no way I was going to miss her wedding.

Because I didn't want the baby to fly so soon, we decided we would drive the eight hours to get there, taking Gracie with us to help look after

Franklin. I was fine with this plan until two nights before our departure when I had a nightmare and woke up with anxiety I couldn't shake. Logically I knew it was unlikely that anything would happen to us on the trip, so I kept my anxiety to myself until John caught me crying later that morning. When I told him about the dream and my feelings, he reassured me that nothing would happen. I could hear Bart's voice saying, "I promise, Jill, you won't lose the boys," but I tried to ignore the voice.

We were to leave Boise at 6:00 am the next day. We had two dogs at the time: Sierra and Josie. After we dropped Sierra at a friend's house, I stopped to visit Martha. "The closer I get to leaving, the more nervous I am," I admitted. Martha tried to calm me, but it was soon time to drop off Josie. With every ounce of my being, I still wanted to get to Jody's wedding. By then bawling and hyperventilating, I finally shouted to John, "There's no way I can get in that car with Franklin!"

John made the phone call to Portland, explaining that I just couldn't handle the drive because of my anxiety, and that I didn't want Jody and her husband Craig to have to focus on my accident and sadness on their special day. As we drove back to Cascade from Boise, I couldn't stop crying and shaking the whole way. My mind was fixated on the accident, the freeway, and the driving time from Boise to Portland: *eight hours*—and the fact that it was eight hours to Venice from Avezzano and eight hours to Portland from Boise was too coincidental for me, making me worry there could be another accident, causing me to lose Franklin, too.

In the safety of our home, I finally settled down. John and I shared a private toast to Jody and Craig, but I still felt regret that my grief had left such a hole in my heart that I had had to miss my good friend's wedding. I had gradually come to accept this reality for myself: when the waves of overwhelming grief washed over me, I had to take care of myself—no matter what—even when it meant hurting people I loved. Because I never wanted to let the grief overwhelm me again, I had to deal with things right when they occurred. Even in my darker periods I understood that, despite my best efforts to control things, grief was sometimes going to be triggered by occurrences. But I had become stronger and better able to handle the resulting feelings. I had learned a process that worked for me: how to stop hurtling down into the grief tunnel.

I had lots of practice. That fall, when Franklin was about six months old, I found out I was pregnant again. I was able to see the baby's heartbeat while John was away on a rafting trip, but shortly after he returned I miscarried. Then I became pregnant again when Franklin was ten months old. We were excited and extremely hopeful for our upcoming doctor's appointment until I started experiencing pain and knew I was having yet another miscarriage. "Let's just go on our trip to the Cascades. I will deal with this when we get home. I'll be fine," I told John. But he wouldn't entertain my suggestion. "Jill, we already have the appointment. You did not have this much pain with the past miscarriages. Let's leave after Doctor Carter says you are okay," he responded. I knew they would need to do an ultrasound, and as I lay there I prayed that I would see something familiar. I didn't. I learned I had a tubal pregnancy and needed emergency surgery. At that point I decided the emotional roller-coaster of pregnancy was too much for me so Franklin would not be having a sibling—except, of course, the two siblings he already had.

The bigger Franklin got, the closer Benjamin and Samuel felt to me. There was no doubt in my mind they were watching over their little brother. Now, Franklin is almost four, getting closer and closer to the age Samuel was at the time of the accident. My sister Jody recently observed that Franklin talks like Benjamin and acts like Samuel, and I think she's right. Like Benjamin, Franklin is curious about everything and feels things deeply. Like Samuel, he can be a bundle of energy that could challenge a mother's ability to keep up.

In Franklin's room, we hung a large photo display of Benjamin, Franklin, and Samuel vertically, with Franklin in the middle, giving me the feeling of the two boys surrounding and protecting their little brother. Franklin also keeps a photo album of Benjamin and Samuel that I created for the room when I gave birth to him. And he has become the keeper of their favorite bears: Benjamin's Bear and Samuel's Barkley. I bought Franklin a giraffe, which is named Penelope, and he loves playing with all three special animals.

My anxiety about another accident occurring sometimes makes me highly protective. For example, I haven't been comfortable allowing Franklin to stay overnight with anyone except Grandma Gracie. I know I can't control everything, but it's not easy to let go. Yet, at the same time, I have noticed a difference in being a mom now. When I would go away overnight with Bart and leave Benjamin and Samuel, they wouldn't be out of my mind for one moment the entire time we were apart. Yet surprisingly when John and I have gone away together to Las Vegas or river rafting, I have been able to put Franklin out of my mind, or at least my minute-by-minute thoughts.

At first this troubled me, making me wonder if I loved Franklin the same way I loved Benjamin and Samuel. Then I realized it was just a coping mechanism. If I allowed myself to experience the deeper feelings of missing Franklin when I was away from him, that would mean also letting in the deeper feelings of missing Benjamin and Samuel on a daily basis, making it difficult to be a good mother to Franklin.

I constantly strive not to let that sense of loss from the past get in the way of loving Franklin in the present. He needs my full attention, and I need to enjoy every minute I have with this delightful and lively boy. We are fortunate to have a large wooded property near our home, and every day I see the joy in Franklin's eyes of playing around here. Of course, I watch out for danger, as any mother would for a child. For example, when we had a bear visitor near our home not long ago, I had John throw a firecracker at it to scare it away. Shooting the bear was not an option because I will not allow a gun in our house, having heard about accidental shootings around Weiser when I was growing up. We also have wolves and coyotes roaming about, so I keep a close eye on Franklin out in the yard. And we always have our dogs with us.

Unlike his mom, Franklin is a natural for country living. He takes after John in that way. For Halloween, which Cascade celebrates with a "trunk and treat," a gathering of vehicles in a parking lot in the center of town, Franklin dressed up as a tractor because his dad owns one. Bart and I used to laugh about everyone in Idaho driving big trucks. Now, here I am with both a big truck and a tractor. I'm pretty sure Bart is laughing.

Since John can handle most of his work from home, he is very involved with day-to-day parenting. It's been gratifying for me to watch him grow in the role of father. "Jill has really taught me how to give the kind of love a child needs," John explains. "She leads by example, by being more affectionate for one thing. I know that Benjamin and Samuel are Franklin's brothers. It feels totally natural to have that connection be a part of our family life."

John has been completely receptive to my desire, and need, to keep many reminders of the boys and Bart in our home, including such items as:

- A framed photo of Benjamin and Samuel playing on the ocean shore one winter day in Italy with temperatures in the 60s
- A framed photo of Benjamin and Samuel with Sarah
- A photo of Samuel at Carnivale wearing a cowboy outfit, Italian style
- A Father's Day sign Benjamin made for Bart that reads: "*Papa sei ottimo*" ("You are magnificent")
- A piece of art made by Samuel that was later bought by Benjamin, who announced, "Mamma, I bought some art" while Samuel said, "Mamma, I sold my volcanoes"
- A music box with various wood inlays that Benjamin had bought in Sorrento
- The piano on which Benjamin took lessons and the guitar we purchased for him in Italy

John also agreed to keep up the tradition of building a secret passageway everywhere I live, this time one that, after pushing a bookshelf at the right spot, opens into a wine cellar stocked with vintage wines we picked up on our travels, as well as bottles that were given to us. At the celebration of our marriage that my sister Jody helped organize, we asked for no gifts except for favorite bottles of wine. In our cellar we keep the signed bottles waiting to be opened when those friends visit.

This is a home that both incorporates parts of my family life with Bart, Benjamin, and Samuel and is clearly the home of John, Franklin, and me. I have to admit that snow is not my passion and here in Cascade, unlike in Boise, we can get a ton of it. But if there is one important lesson I learned living in Italy it is this: As long as you have your family around you, you can find happiness wherever you are. And with my husband and son surrounding me, that is what I am committed to doing every day.

Chapter 16
The Question
Where Does God Fit In?

LOSING THE FIVE MOST IMPORTANT PEOPLE in my life and struggling with grief has reconfigured how and why I connect with God and where it takes me. When I was young, friends would often tell me, "I wish I had your faith." Today, I can honestly say that after all the pain and suffering, all the darkness, all the periods of heartache and hopelessness, I still have that faith. I feel a very strong presence of God in my life. I couldn't imagine taking this journey of grief recovery without that presence.

Yet, like everything else in my life, my relationship with God has been deeply impacted by the accident. As reflected in many of my journal entries and my responses to the exercises in the *Grief Recovery Workbook* that I relied on at the convent in Italy, I have had many tough questions for God and about God. As I have sought answers, I have experienced the role of God in my life evolving.

I grew up in a Lutheran family, though to me organized religion is just a tool to help support faith and provide a feeling of community. What matters more is the strength of faith in God and how consistently we connect with him in our day-to-day lives. I always had that kind of faith. Faith helped sustain me after my parents divorced when I was a teenager. Faith helped hold me together in my early adult years when I wandered from place to place and pursuit to pursuit, searching for purpose and direction. Faith helped give me the conviction that the ring I coveted at JC Penney would someday be placed on my finger by the man of my dreams.

A church is what brought Bart and me together. We met at that singles event my mom organized through The Beautiful Savior Church and later got married there. I even worked for the church for a while. More importantly, Bart and I shared a faith that God was a critical part of everything we did. We made choices together guided by God.

When Benjamin was born, we decided that we were no longer a fit for The Beautiful Savior Church and began shopping for a new church. That's when I discovered Community of Life. It was a Lutheran Evangelical church but more liberal than the church I had been attending while growing up in Weiser. The church had a lively band and welcomed attendees wearing shorts and T-shirts. Bart wasn't so sure about that part, preferring a more formal feel at church. When Bart suggested that we join a different church in downtown Boise, we interviewed the pastors of both churches. When Pastor Mark from Community of Life left our house after his visit, I was so touched that I cried. "Please give this church one year, Bart," I said.

Bart agreed, and for me there could not have been a better church for us. The openness, nonjudgmental attitude, and fun atmosphere I experienced there made me feel loved, accepted, and joyous. Pastor Mark had an ability to put a Bible passage into the context of current events and real life issues in a way that other pastors I had known could not. And the biggest benefit of all was that I felt God's presence whenever I was there. Everything we did at Community of Life was about strengthening our relationship with God.

Bart and I quickly found our place in the church community. We were regulars at a Bible study group during the week, and I taught Sunday school to kids ages three and up. I remember our Easter crafts projects: making a mosaic cross, decorating a flower pot and then planting a flower in it as an example of how new life begins, making table decorations with lights for a big Christmas party. Once a month Pastor Mark led an event for older kids, ages six and up, so when we left for Italy we were looking forward to having Benjamin join in those events when we returned. At one point, Bart was president and Mom served as treasurer of the church, which grew to about one hundred members. Sadly, while we were in Italy the church began to dissolve. Pastor Mark moved away, and Bart's presence was missed in the leadership group. Jonathan and Sheri from Micron, who also had been active leaders there, left for Italy, too. Bart and I were beginning to question whether we would stay with the church when we moved back.

Then the accident created an even greater strain on the church. Mom and Bart were not there to help keep things going, and neither Jody nor I were involved any longer, neither of us emotionally or physically inclined to attend. No one had the energy to recruit new members while mourning. Eventually the Community of Life merged with another Boise church before ultimately dissolving.

When I came back from Italy physically and mentally battered in the spring of 2002, I knew I needed support from somewhere. I also knew I would not find it at my church. It would need to come directly through my personal relationship with God.

Before the accident, I believed that all you had to do was put your faith in God and you could face anything in your path. I took to heart what they said about how God wouldn't give you anything you couldn't handle. From the time Benjamin and Samuel were very young, I had fears of losing them, and I tried to trust in God that he would not allow that to happen. The last thing I remember in that rental car outside Bologna was praying for their safety. But it didn't work. Or God wasn't listening. Or he didn't care enough about me. Or I hadn't proven myself enough to him. Or something.

After the accident, I questioned whether God existed because my God would not have allowed this to happen. This questioning initiated a wrestling match with God. It was a period when I felt betrayed by everyone and everything that was part of the accident, often including God. I wrote one day in my journal:

God expects so much of me. He has the power to make things different and easier. I must not be important because I'm just left to keep plugging along, hoping to miraculously join them in heaven.

It took me many weeks and months of agonizing soul-searching to get beyond that attitude. When other people would say God had a plan for me, to me that implied that this plan had somehow included the accident in which everyone I loved had been killed so I could fulfill God's destiny in some preordained way—a view that didn't make sense to me.

I had to come to understand that the accident just happened, that God hadn't created it. He hadn't waved his hand over the autostrada and made the semi truck plow into us. Instead, what I ultimately came to believe was that God had given me the support and tools to get healthy *after* the accident.

I've thought a lot about how this works. I notice how people so often pray for cancer sufferers to get better. I respect their beliefs and understand their needs, but I don't believe that's how God operates. I think he is there to help people with cancer deal with the suffering and to help their families become better able to face whatever may come—a view reflected in my journal:

> *You are no different from anyone else, Jill. God didn't choose you to deal with this tragedy because you are strong. This is not his doing. This happened for no understandable reason. But God will give you the tools to help yourself. Through everything you are experiencing, God is holding you, whether you feel him or not. You can get through this, not because you are the only one who can but because you have to.*
>
> *God has given me so much: the ability to get healthy again; the desire to survive and be happy. Just because things don't happen at my pace doesn't mean God has abandoned me. Quite the opposite. Where would I be if I didn't believe in him? Angry, bitter, with no desire to live, empty. I can honestly say I am full of love and happiness. Yes, I have fears—fear of losing my ability, fear of failing God. But I do have God. And with him all is possible!*

There was another side to my wrestling match with God that I initially struggled to reconcile. Maybe God hadn't caused the accident and made my loved ones die, but since the accident happened by fate why couldn't he have allowed me to die in it and stay with my family? Or if surviving the accident was such a miracle, as many people around me would insist, shouldn't God let me know the reason I was supposed to survive so I could focus on that purpose?

Eventually I reached a peace with this question as well. I decided that God probably does have a plan for me now but I may never become aware of it. Instead, I may just live it. The strongest indications I have is that this plan would somehow include giving to others and trying to make a difference in the world. I always felt at home in endeavors such as volunteering for Make-A-Wish Foundation or teaching at the orphanage in Italy. And my heart would rise when I studied the examples of Mother Teresa, or Pope John Paul, or even Oprah. Now I felt that I wanted to help people, which would surely be God's work and a way to express gratitude to him for helping me get through my grief.

For a while, I wondered if I might find another church that would support my healing and enhance my connection to God. Sometime after the accident I met with a pastor from a nondenominational church who also happened to be named Mark. I explained why I was reluctant to go back to any church and expressed my fear that I would hear the dreaded message: "All you have to do is trust in God and everything will be okay. God does not give you anything you can't handle." Yet I felt at ease talking to Mark, so I asked him if it might be possible for me to have visits with him outside his church. Soon we were meeting regularly for coffee at Moxie Java, and Mark didn't try to persuade me to reconsider joining his church. "God does not require that you go to a church," he said. "That may not be a healthy environment for you right now. God is still with you, but church may never be a place God will direct you to go again. As long as you are open and hear what he wants you to do, it will be the right choice."

Hearing those words was a great comfort to me. To my mind, organized religion is a man-made entity anyway while our faith is not man made but from God. Religion is a tool God has provided to strengthen our faith, and God has given us all kinds of tools, including the people we love. I believe, for example, that God put Bart, John, Kelly, and Carla in my life. Carla and I share many views about faith, especially that faith is not about religion. Often she would tell me that Bart and the boys could still communicate with me if I opened my heart to them, and she urged me to talk to them, which I've done in my own way.

I find that I don't need to call myself Lutheran or even Christian anymore. I've learned that there are many different ways for people to express their belief in a higher being. We're all praying to the same God, no matter the denomination or religion. God knows what works best for each of us. I'm more focused on seeking to discover what God wants me to do, and in some ways God has told me what he needs from me. I pray to God for direction in most everything I do, just like I did the night John proposed in the hot tub.

In my current marriage, it's been a challenge for me that John does not openly express a belief in God. When Franklin was born, I worried how it would be if his dad didn't have faith, and I even wondered if John might try to dissuade me from teaching our son about God. Fortunately, that has not happened. And I believe God will show himself to John when he's ready. I have tried to force this a few times, at which point I would hear God say, "I know what is best."

From early on in my grieving process, people would sometimes advise me to read the Book of Job, as en example of human suffering and perseverance. When it was first suggested, I scoffed and muttered under my breath, "Oh, even Job didn't have it as bad as me!" But over time I did read the Book of Job, looking for any messages for me and wondering if perhaps God really was trying to speak to me through it. I found I could relate to several aspects of the book: the fact that Job went through so much pain and others blamed him for how he responded to it at times; the fact that Job had a lot of questions for God, including questions of belief, and God still stood by him; and the fact that God finally told Job what he needed from him, which was to teach people about God because they weren't understanding.

I sense that perhaps God wants me to remind others, through example, of what he wants from us: love, nonjudgmental compassion, and more. I also believe that he is hoping I will share my experience of this tragedy as a way of illustrating how God helps us through hard times—all kinds of difficult or painful experiences—and that he's not "making" us go through them. I will continue to be open to the possibility that God is directing me to a greater purpose and do my best to follow his guidance.

Chapter 17
The Reality
Merging Two Separate Lives into One

OVER TIME MY RELATIONSHIP WITH SHARON, the counselor who was so helpful during my recovery, had evolved beyond her being my professional therapist. She had become a friend I could rely on in many aspects of my life. When we talked, there was no frivolous small talk but only conversation that got to the heart of matters because she knew me better than anyone else. One day I confided in her my desire to share my experiences with the aim of helping others facing grief. Because she was a grief expert, I figured she'd have ideas about speaking prospects for me. "I think I'm ready to start speaking in public about my experience," I told her. "Can you help me find somewhere to get started with that?" I knew speaking engagements would stir up emotions related to the past—the struggles and pain, as well as the healing and joy. Yet I also believed that I could make a difference in the lives of others who were facing their own kind of grief, or to those who assist people seeking to recover from some loss or tragedy.

"I have someplace in mind as a possibility," Sharon responded, to my delight. Soon she put me in touch with her friend Rebecca Hauder, who was teaching a class on grief at Boise State University. The class was a mix of students and professionals, including counselors and coaches, who either regularly or occasionally helped people in the grieving process.

After quickly agreeing to speak to the class, I spent a lot of time praying to God to give me the strength to speak in front of people. John was a big support in getting me ready, listening to what I had written for my talk and giving me valuable feedback. More importantly, he held me when the pain from having to relive my experiences poured out.

I recalled the song I put in my first music journal, "Life after Bart"— "One Moment More" by Mindy Smith—and considered it the perfect background music for the slide show of my family that would be part of my talk. When I was satisfied with my planned presentation, I was excited but also nervous. Practicing my speech in front of my neighbors and hearing their positive encouragement helped spur me on.

I hoped to take my audience from the top of a giant wave—the life of a woman in excellent health and surrounded by love—to the moment the wave came crashing down, causing a riptide to pull the woman underwater, and then finally to rippling water—the woman embracing life in the midst of an enduring sense of pain and loss. I wanted to address the critical questions: How do you make room for the pain to come in and still somehow survive without your loved one? How do you climb back up from the grief tunnel to rejoin the flow of life?

I knew that giant wave well. I understood all too clearly what it was like to spend months and years trapped in that riptide waiting for the undertow to push me back to the surface. And I had slowly learned what can work to break through the surface and gasp for the breath I needed so badly. Now I was ready to walk other people through it.

On the day of my speech, after introducing myself I invited the audience to take out pen and paper, saying, "Please write down the five most important people in your life, such as your family members and friends. Take a moment to picture those people in your life…in your home. Now I would like to introduce you to the five most important people in my life."

As I displayed photos of my family one by one, I commented on their qualities and their importance to me:

"My mom—she is extremely funny. She loves to play golf. She lives for her 'grandbabies.' She is the person who has taught me unconditional love and to have faith in God.

"My niece Sarah—Sarah, also my goddaughter, loves to play practical jokes, like placing plastic bugs in ice cube trays. Her smile and laughter bring me joy every day.

"My husband Bart—the love of my life! The first time I laid eyes on him I knew he had stolen my heart. A few times a week we play Scrabble before bed. Knowing that Bart was valedictorian of his high school class of five hundred, it gives me great pleasure when I beat him. Some nights when there's music in the background Bart reaches for my hand to dance with me in the middle of our living room. He is the man who has taught me what true love is.

"My son Benjamin —Benjamin is the most giving soul! He created a way to raise money for the poor, planning a menu and entertainment. His motto is 'Mamma, you can make art out of anything.'

"My son Samuel—Samuel lights up the room when he enters! Samuel's motto is 'Mamma, can I have some candy?' He asks this question every morning, convinced I will break at some point.

"On March 25, 2002, all five of the most important people in my life died."

From there I started the slide show of their pictures with Mindy Smith's song "One Moment More" playing in the background. I shared my story, doing my best to make it through the hard parts, including my attempted suicide. I then took them through my grief recovery and brought them into my present-day life. Near the end of my talk I shared this reflection: "Today I live parallel lives. One is the life of a person struggling endlessly with grief, the other is the life of a wife and mother loving each day she has with her family. From the outside, it may appear as though my life is fully back on track. But the reality is that every minute of every day I struggle to live as a normal person. Happiness is always my goal, but on some days happiness is beyond my reach."

The idea that after the accident I was living parallel lives had resonated with me for a long time. In the beginning of my recovery process, it felt as though my old self was watching an unrecognizable character struggle to survive. This character felt disconnected from me, harsh, unaware of my true condition, and unable to articulate my feelings. I felt as though two different people existed in my body, which perhaps was partly true. However, through many years of soul-searching and study I have learned how to merge the two separate lives into one livable existence:

☞ Jill, the woman with a loving husband and son who strives to be a loyal and supportive friend and seeks new and bolder ways to reach out to others in need.

☞ Jill, the grieving soul who screeches in shock every time she touches the burning memories of her past and who suffers through days wondering if she will survive.

My grief also seems to occur on two distinct tracks. On the one hand, I am keenly aware of my feelings about loss of Bart, Benjamin, and Samuel, thinking about them almost nonstop, talking about them frequently, and used to the pain I may experience in connection with memories of them. On the other hand, my feelings of loss of Mom and Sarah somehow remain much more inaccessible, as if too hot to handle. Consequently, I have made a special effort to face memories of Mom and Sarah to fully experience this loss and to better understand their roles in my life. For example, in sorting through reminders of Mom, I came across an Identity Book I had been assigned to write in school during my teenage years, which included the following entry from my mom: "Jill's greatest strength is her kindness to everyone…seldom moody…sincere loving person, hopes to do modeling, acting, music. I am proud to be her mother."

We were very close throughout my childhood, and I could see how much she suffered after her divorce. I remember evenings when she would have to serve us popcorn for dinner because we couldn't afford more. Dad did not always pay child support, not because he was trying to hurt her but because she had always managed their money and now he was struggling to budget his finances. Mom didn't have a job outside the home until she was fifty-five because Dad would not let her work. When she did get a job, she loved the independence it gave her, and as she became more comfortable in jewelry sales and then real estate her confidence soared. She took great pride in being able to buy her own house in Boise, and when her relationship with Dick moved toward marriage she kept her own money. She also did many things to bolster my self-esteem. I remember how, after Bart and I got engaged, she and Dick hosted a party for Bart's parents. Mom, aware of how insecure I felt because our family had never been nearly as formal as Bart's, insisted on preparing a proper seven-course meal, as if to say, "Jill, we are just as good as anybody else."

After my family moved to Italy, I cherished my regular phone calls and daily email exchanges with Mom. In one email, not long before that fateful trip when the accident occurred, I wrote: "*Vorrei la mamma*" ("I would like my mom").

And she was so determined to see us, flying just four days after 9/11 and telling others in our family, "I have to go be with my baby."

In my journaling through music, while I have been able to prepare a CD about Bart and the boys to face the raw emotions stirred by the memories, I have not been able to prepare a CD about Mom. I could try to argue that it's too difficult because she was not much into music herself, but the reality is that I've had so many losses I haven't been capable of fully facing the loss of her. In fact, sometimes I have caught myself running downstairs and saying, "I need to call Mom today." For a long time, I simply didn't allow myself to face the reality that she was gone. I had been away from her most of the time while living in Italy anyway so, as silly as it may sound, I clung to the idea that I was on vacation and that's why I was away from her. While my logical side recognized the need to grieve the loss of all five people in my life, my emotional side was so aware of how painful it has been to allow in the loss of Bart and the boys that it was reluctant to allow in the loss of Mom. However, occasionally such feelings seeped through anyway. One day John recognized my familiar sadness and asked what was wrong, probably assuming I'd launch into the usual talk of how I missed Bart, Benjamin, and Samuel. But I said, "I just miss my mom today," with tears welling.

On that last trip to Italy, I wanted so badly for her to have some rest and enjoy the beauty of the places in Italy she had not seen during her first visit. Mom was a surprisingly worldly person, but during her first time in Italy she had been so excited she had acted like a big kid. Had Mom lived,

I was looking forward to her retiring so she wouldn't have to work so hard and would have more opportunities to travel with Aunt Doris as they had done in Italy. And, of course, I was also looking forward to having her watch her "grandbabies" grow up.

Another area I am working through is relating to my new home with John and Franklin. One part of me appreciates the fact that we are surrounded by nature and beauty and knows that the rural quiet could help me feel more peaceful and slow down so I fully immerse myself in this new family life. But the other part of me rebels against it, making me want less solitude and more options for activities and interactions with people.

Even though I keep reminding myself that I can still accomplish the things that are important for me in Cascade and that the quiet works for a while, I slip back to cursing it and find something to escape to instead of tuning in to what the quiet is calling me to do.

I expressed this conflict in a journal entry:

This change of having John and Franklin in my life and living here has been awesome, but it still has thrown me. When I was living alone in Boise, I busied myself, hoping to find a life. Well, I found one but it's not in Boise. It is here in Cascade with my family. I want this life. I am just scared to face it because it means leaving more behind. Living on the southeast part of Boise gave me a chance to connect with Bart and Benjamin and Samuel because we lived in that area. I felt connected to Mom and Sarah there, too. Now, living in a small town in the boonies has nothing to do with them. Bart would go insane here.

Living and working here is certainly a challenge, but I need to face it. I need to find enjoyment in my new surroundings. Everything I need and desire is here; I just have to to tap into it. I can travel and see friends in Boise when I want to. I can still dress well and enjoy nice things here. Culture, books, art…those won't go away unless I let them. I can still accomplish the things that are important to me: my ceramics, walking, biking, relearning the trumpet, reading, writing, etc. There were negatives to living in Italy, but I found a way to embrace the positives there. I can do that here, too.

One way I cope with too much quiet is to escape by making myself busy. John gets angry because I won't just stay in one place, even to watch TV. I've always got to be cleaning, doing laundry—anything to keep my mind occupied. Even though it's a beautiful drive up from Boise through a canyon to Cascade, I can't enjoy it because I lose cell phone service and start getting frightened about what may run through my mind. I am too afraid that slowing down for even a minute will open the floodgates to inescapable feelings. I sometimes tell myself that if I stay busy, I can just outrun the pain and confusion. Even when I go back to Boise I'm constantly busy—always visiting with friends, shopping, eating out, or doing a million things around the house. When I lived in my house there full time, I used to start gardening at 6:00 am, or work on a ceramics project late at night when I wasn't sleeping. Kelly would come over and say, "You're accomplishing so much before I even get out of bed." Actually, this was because of my fear of inactivity. It is much easier to busy yourself than to face your fears and grief head-on. Even while writing this book I have had to struggle with the reluctance to face my fears and grief, with one part of me unwilling to risk reopening old wounds. "Write, Jill," one voice would say. And then the other voice would rebut: "What? And risk going back to that deep darkness of hell? What if I get there and I can't find my way back? I won't be able to be a good mom to Franklin."

Yet another dynamic with which I continue to struggle is my difficulty interacting with people after the accident. From early on I have wanted people's support and connection, but then when they have done their best to offer support or bring me into the flow of life, I have often turned away. I've compared this experience to being asked to join in a conga dance: I watch people going around, seemingly enjoying themselves. Every so often a person grabs my arm to pull me in, assuming that I will be happier if I participate. When that tug comes, I may allow myself to be swept up in the action briefly, but as soon as possible I head off to the restroom or grab a drink, letting the dance go on without me, letting life pass me by.

While I am gradually getting better at interacting with people and letting them inside my world, sometimes when people approach me I still get caught in an awkward mix of gratitude for their interest and irritation at them for not understanding my situation. I know they're trying to help when they ask: "How are you doing? What are you doing? How do you fill up your days?" If that happened once a week, with one person asking, I could handle it, maybe even welcome it. But often such questions are fired at me every day, and since I'm often peppering myself with the same questions I get battle fatigue.

I usually try to answer them, with my responses varying from person to person and moment to moment, depending on my ever-changing mood. What I do occasionally, and should do more regularly, is let others know that the best thing anyone can do to show support for me is to talk about *themselves*. I have twenty-four hours to think about and analyze my life. It has become my "job," and everyone needs a break from their job. It's a gift to hear about someone else's day-to-day activities or even their problems.

Of course, with the most trusted people close to me I have not been as conflicted about receiving their love and support. In recent years that circle has come to include Bart's mother LaVonne. After the accident, she and Duane moved to Eagle to be closer to Todd and Lisa and their kids, which meant they were also closer to us. I still very much consider them family, and they treat John like a son and Franklin as their grandson. LaVonne writes to Franklin so he will get mail, with stickers and lots of love, just as she used to do for Benjamin and Samuel. Duane and John go for beers sometimes. In many ways, LaVonne has become my mother figure. No one can replace my mom, but LaVonne listens to me and loves me. I seek her advice at times, and we sometimes cry over how much we both miss Bart. I am so grateful that LaVonne and Duane have stepped in and cared for me while my parents haven't been able to.

It has also helped me to express my needs in advance of gatherings where people might ask too many questions concerning my well-being—as I did in the hospital during the time of Franklin's birth when I posted a letter on my door telling the story of my accident. I did a similar thing when getting ready for my twentieth high school reunion at Weiser High. I only planned to attend the events for one day, though it was a two-hour drive each way. Even in that short time, though, I knew that many people would ask me about the accident and come up to me with twenty variations of "How are you doing now?" So I wrote and mailed to all my classmates the following letter:

> Hi, everyone! I hope to see you all soon. I wanted to let you all know about my accident before we see each other. It will be more fun during the reunion if I get all the depressing stuff out of the way first. I am so thankful for your thoughts and prayers following the accident, and even now. I know we all have been through some tough times in our lives. These things will never go away, but we learn to deal with them. I have found that it helps me be the one in control of when and where I decide to discuss it.
>
> So here's the deal: If I talk about the accident, it is because I want to not because I felt forced to. When I tell stories about them, just realize I am happiest when I share and not sad about my loss. Yes, I know what happened sucks, but please don't put me on a pedestal. I have been through something I pray none of you will have to go through, but we all know pain. We can't feel what others have been through; we just know it must hurt. All any of us who have suffered a loss can do is share ways we step through our grief. Sometimes, if one of us is lucky something might work to help us.

In addition to utilizing these methods of controlling how I interact with people about my grief, when people I don't know are going to visit us John often preps them on my story before they arrive so I don't have to see shock and pain shoot across their faces. And when he sees a conversation slipping toward my danger zone he changes the subject, being very protective of me.

At the same time, there are occasions when I actually do want to talk about my painful losses and grief, especially if I sense it could be helpful to other people. So I keep a lookout for such situations where my teaching may be useful. I have a longing to help others deal with their pain of loss, which in return will also help me find a greater sense of purpose.

When I talk with others about the grief experience, I always start with this essential reminder: no one's grief is the same as anyone else's grief, although hopefully some people may benefit from what others have experienced. I also remind listeners to keep in mind the fact that the grieving process may never actually end. It may, instead, simply evolve and along the way manifest discouraging moments when it may appear that the griever has not really progressed much. Evidence of such a relapse is reflected in a journal entry I made two days after what would have been Samuel's eleventh birthday:

Today is Sunday, September 14. Did I give myself a chance to acknowledge Samuel's birthday two days ago? Yes, and I was sad. But I held back the tears, fought the desire to pound something, and resisted the urge to scream at the top of my voice. I allowed my laughter to shine on the happy memories. And then the questions arose: How could my little four-year-old boy be eleven? What would he be like if he were here? I know he would be so very handsome. But would his hair be the same color? His eyes? How tall would he be? I am positive his laughter would still light up the room, but would it be deep like his daddy's yet? Oh, why can't I know my son anymore?

A few more birthdays for Benjamin and Samuel have come and gone since then, but the questions pop up every time. And it doesn't take a birthday to rekindle the feeling of missing them and wondering: Did my life with them really exist? Were they real? Sometimes when I look at the photos of Benjamin, he feels like a person in a dream. I can't feel his warmth, his love. And sometimes I hardly even remember Samuel.

Even though being around Franklin, seeing how adorable and smart he is, gives me such joy, it sometimes hurts to watch him because he reminds me of Benjamin and Samuel, and I become afraid of losing Franklin, too. When Franklin sees me looking glum, he sometimes asks me about it. "Why do you look so sad, Mom?" he says.

"I just miss Benjamin and Samuel," I respond.

"But I'm here, Mom," he replies.

"Yes, and that makes me so happy!" I answer.

I don't hide my parallel life from my son. When I put Franklin to bed at night, I sing the same songs I used to sing to Benjamin and Samuel, and I mention all three of their names. But, not wanting to jinx myself, I have changed the words in the last line of "You Are My Sunshine" to "And when I woke, dear, I was so happy, because I held you all day long."

I explain to others how my grieving process has resulted in having two parallel lives by saying I'm living in my new life and still living in my old life, too. I just seek to accept that I'm simply living two separate lives. I still talk to Bart sometimes, and I ask the boys to protect Franklin. I also let John and Franklin know how much I love them as often as I can. It all makes for a delicate balancing act. It doesn't mean that I can't appreciate a beautiful sunset, or a fresh snowfall, or a leisurely glass of fine wine, or the wonders of a deep and meaningful friendship. It doesn't mean I can't laugh, or that I can't love. And it may just be that with every passing year, or every passing day, I can have all of that just a bit more often.

Chapter 18
Finding Purpose for the Future

WHILE IT'S SCARY FOR ME TO PLAN or even talk about the far-off future, I'm taking steps to discover and fulfill my purpose in this life rather than letting grief defeat me. One way I have been assessing my new life purpose is by determining and claiming my new identity. I can trace my changes in identity by considering the many different names I have had over the years. I was born Jill Ann Hill. When I was married to Bart, I was Jill Ann Kraft. Now that I'm married to John, I am Jill Kraft Thompson, so my full name is Jill Ann Hill Kraft Thompson. But, after watching the movie *The Gladiator* during my healing retreat at the convent a year after the accident, I adopted yet another name, Jillius, after Maximus, the hero of a story from the days of the Roman Empire, with whom I identified. In the movie, Maximus, a loyal and courageous general who never loses a battle, finds himself suddenly grieving the killings of his wife and young son. After Maximus is betrayed, he is forced to live under another identity as a slave and gladiator. At first he rebels against his plight and yearns for only one thing: to join his wife and son in the afterlife. This will happen, he is told by a wise slave, but not until Maximus has fulfilled his purpose in life. This realization spurs him to call upon his deepest reserves to overcome his trials and tribulations, supported by a woman who loves him. After he avenges the killings of his family and his beloved ruler, and acts to restore Rome to the people, he dies, comforted by the last words he hears uttered by the woman who understands: "Go to them...." Like Maximus, Jillius will someday "go to them," will join Bart, Benjamin, Samuel, Mom, and Sarah in heaven. But also like Maximus Jillius strives to find and fulfill her purpose in this life now. Just as naming my apparatus Beatrice gave me strength until I could get her off me, naming myself

Jillius has helped give me strength when tired and discouraged, knowing my grief will be with me until my dying day.

Meanwhile, living with John has opened many new doors for me. In our early days, he coaxed me out of my cocoon enough to walk to the end of the driveway when my grief was keeping me in bed. As the years have gone by, he has introduced me to many of his favorite outdoor pursuits. I haven't taken to snowmobiling as much as he would like, but I have joined him on a camping outing aboard a cataraft going down the Owyhee River. Together we have joined what we all call "The Redneck Yacht Club," a group of folks in the McCall area who tie their boats together and just have a good time socializing. We also recently invested in working with a fitness coach together, and we've taken advantage of the snowy climate to teach Franklin to ski.

Yet, to be honest, this is also a marriage that has had its trials and tribulations. We have faced some tough challenges and wrestled with some thorny issues, the same kind of marital conflict most couples encounter at some point of their union, even Bart and I. Yet John and I both have summoned the strength to stay together and have attained a new kind of mutual respect. Almost from the beginning I would laugh with John that Bart probably picked John out for me. After all, they both came from the Seattle area. At times I've playfully, or not so playfully, shaken my head and added, "and I would like to have a little talk with Bart about that choice!" Of course, I also feel deep gratitude for the ways in which John has supported me in my grief recovery, and I've taken great pleasure in watching him become an amazing dad to Franklin. I love them both deeply and want so much for them.

Despite my reluctance to plan for the future, recently I was able to discuss Franklin's schooling with John. The time when he will attend kindergarten is fast approaching, and we live in an area where we've had to drive forty-five minutes one way just so he could get to a suitable preschool. With school opportunities so limited, we have considered moving to ensure Franklin gets a better education. John was gracious enough to consider possibly returning full time to Boise, as long as our new home has enough acreage for his outdoor "toys." I considered that offer since I am a city girl at heart, but then realized that although I would not have chosen to live in the mountains north of Boise, this is where I belong. In Boise I'd be back to constant activity that would likely help me avoid facing my grief head-on. Just as important, I know how much John and Franklin love it up here. Seeing how much joy it brings them has helped me embrace this area as part of my life purpose for the future.

We have also had to deal with other trials and tribulations beyond emotional and mental pain and confusion. The accident resulted in two lawsuits. The first lawsuit, related to the driver of the semi truck and his trucking company, was resolved after many years of ongoing tussle. The second lawsuit, pertaining to the driver of the US Army truck, is only now, ten years after the accident, finally reaching the finish line. This second lawsuit has been even more complicated because we had to deal with the governments of both Italy and the United States. Trying to get anything done in Italian courts in any reasonable time frame is like climbing a mountain with weights on your feet. Also, for some reason the US government can plead the fifth amendment when an accident happens outside the country, and even though we are US citizens we have no ability to see their reports. So although no disagreements have occurred about who the responsible parties are, I have been forced to wait patiently for some resolution.

Now that the final decree and settlement are at hand, I've also found myself wanting to reach out to Massimilliano Monte, the driver of the semi truck, and Anthony Garza, the driver of the US Army truck. I have no malice toward them, but I do need closure. After searching unsuccessfully for some way to reach them via the Internet, I wrote them the following letter, asking for God's guidance in writing them, and gave it to my attorney:

Dear Massimilliano and Anthony,
My name is Jill Kraft Thompson. I am writing to you both to let you know how I am. This tragedy has affected so many people, including the two of you. My hope is that if I share my thoughts and feelings with you it will

not only help but strengthen you. I cannot imagine how this accident has impacted your lives. Even I think about how things might have been different if I would not have stopped for lunch or if we could have left the hotel in Venice earlier. I try hard to make these five deaths not to have occurred. If only we could go back in time! I do not know that I will ever have the peace of mind of knowing exactly what happened. I have found that two people can go through the exact same experience yet have completely different views of it. What I do know is that no one wanted this tragedy to occur. And I forgive both of you for anything you did or did not do that resulted in these deaths.

I think of you both often, not with anger or hate but with compassion and concern. I see people go through events in their lives without the strength to overcome obstacles. They turn to alcohol, drugs, and other things to lessen their pain or forget their troubles. This affects not only them but the people surrounding them. I remember the day I made the decision to become healthy after the accident. It has been a long road of soul-searching and grief. Yet through my hard work I am successful most days at being healthy and happy. I have a loving husband and a beautiful little boy! But the most amazing success is that I can look into a mirror and recognize the person looking back.

My hope is that this letter finds you both in successful, happy lives. If instead this finds you in chaos, please, for me and those who care for you, summon the strength you need to make a change. You are both in my thoughts and prayers now and throughout my life!

Take care,

Jill

Writing that letter gave me a great sense of peace, especially since I did it only days before the tenth anniversary of the accident. I had my attorney send it soon after I got the call that the judgment had not been appealed. That news arrived on March 12—Bart's forty-eighth birthday. It almost felt as if Bart had given me a birthday present by ending the lawsuit on that day, yet the excitement at hearing this resolution was tinged with sadness about its nature.

In the years during the lawsuits, they have been a cloud hanging overhead that kept many details of the crash too close for comfort. Long ago I had decided not to visit Italy again until this last lawsuit was completely resolved. Italy is still where I feel closest to Bart, Benjamin, and Samuel, but I haven't been back since 2005 because the recovery process I endure every time I go back has become even longer and more difficult due to the lawsuit.

And while initially I had no memory of the details of the accident from the moment I prayed to God for our safety before falling asleep in the minivan until the moment I woke up in the hospital, now through my dreams memories of that day are slowly returning. The first significant dream concerning the accident occurred while John and I were on a trip in Alaska. I don't remember much of the action of this nightmare, but I do remember the smell: the horrid stench of burning flesh, strong enough to make me sick to my stomach and wake up screaming hysterically. After John did his best to calm me, he said, "I don't think I can help you with this one. You need to call Sharon." As I explained the dream to Sharon, I kept shouting, "I don't want to see them all dead!" We talked for over an hour, and she helped me get through it. Sharon told me that I probably did see the accident but didn't want to remember it, which is perfectly natural. It's also natural that my memory would begin to reveal some of what I had buried, little by little.

Another nightmare about the accident occurred more recently, but this dream was a montage of past and present events. In the dream, I was on the freeway with John and Franklin when a semi truck passed us in slow motion. I heard the screeching, my scream, and the other horrendous sounds of our past accident. I knew what was happening and also that all I had to do was look into the rearview mirror to see the details of the accident, but I chose not to look. I interpreted this dream as a reminder that although I still don't want to see, I need to understand that what is revealed through these chilling dreams may actually be part of my healing process.

I have also had other related dreams. Weeks later, I dreamt of Benjamin one night and Bart the next. In the dream about Benjamin, he was stolen from me for five hours, and when I got him back he was not able to explain what had happened but did say that he missed me. In the dream about Bart, we both knew he was gone, but we were able to be to-gether and even laugh, hug, and kiss! I asked him questions, which he an-swered in a way that made sense in the dream, though I couldn't remember what was said when I awoke. He teased me about John and told me that where he was he could talk to me but not see me.

As the passage of time has permitted retrieval of lost memories about the accident, it has also given me greater awareness of how quickly the young people in my life have been growing up during the interim of my grief recovery. When I was deep in grief, I kept my distance from chil-dren anywhere near the ages of Benjamin and Samuel because I was always afraid that if I got close to someone young I would be overwhelmed with sadness and fear. That meant not really knowing my nephew Jack, as well as Kelly and Martha's kids, and many others. It's even been a struggle letting Jody and Paul's new little boy Jace get too close, although when he wouldn't call me Aunt Jill but only Miss Jill, because he did not really care for ants, I smiled, remembering how his sister Sarah used to call me Puppy. Now I feel badly about having distanced myself from these young individuals, but finally I have begun to reconnect with them. As a result, it has been amaz-ing to discover that Kelly's daughter Sadie and Martha's daughters Sara and Laura are all teenagers, and Jack's voice is low now. Recently, when I no-ticed that Laura was having a difficult time with family issues, I invited her for a pedicure and a little "girl talk." It felt good to reach out—maybe I am one less loss for her now.

Laura, the girl a year younger than Benjamin whom he wanted to "marry," is now fifteen. So Benjamin would be sixteen and getting his driver's license. Another reminder of Benjamin's age, had he lived, came when Diletta, Benjamin's classmate at Sacro Coure and the girl I had once considered adopting, recently contacted me through Facebook, letting me know that she has grown to be a beautiful young woman.

Recently I observed Samuel's fourteenth birthday. As I tried to figure out what to do for the day, I vividly remembered the last birthday I had been able to celebrate with Samuel, when he turned four. That day Bart and I took the boys to Rome, where they bought new shirts at the Disney store for Samuel's big party. Samuel loved Buzz Light Year, so his present was a plastic Buzz about a foot tall. We had a cake made with a toy truck on it, but my Italian instructions to make this a little boy's cake must not have been understood because the tasty cake had been soaked in alcohol. At least Samuel got to eat plenty of candy. And, as always, Benjamin helped his brother feel very special.

Now, in honoring Samuel's fourteenth birthday, it was his brother Franklin who stepped forward. Franklin made a point to call Samuel on "his" phone and send him love and kisses. The day before the birthday my nerves were raw. I could feel Samuel—his soft little cheek, his tight squeeze around my neck. Then I remembered that Franklin was almost as old now as Samuel was back then. Sue had saved Samuel's Buzz Light Year with "Samuel" written on the bottom foot and given it to Franklin on his third birthday. Though it's still scary to think about Franklin's future, I know it will continue to unfold and that I'll be there with him.

I know I can't protect myself against all losses in the days and years ahead. Things happen. People close to us die. A while ago I was contacted by Sister Carla, who let me know that Sister Pasquina had passed away. While I was saddened to hear the news, I found comfort in the image of Sister Pasquina joining Samuel in heaven. When they hug there, they will be able to speak the same language and finally understand each other. Recently I heard that Steve Appleton, the CEO of Micron, also had died. Right after the accident Steve had been very helpful in working with Brian and Wayne to take care of the needs of my family and friends. And some years ago I had to face the loss of another dog when Rue, who had succeeded Ritter, perished in a wood piling outside our home.

Yes, losses will come, but, as the passage of time has demonstrated, the future may also bring new people and opportunities into this new life of mine. John and Franklin top that list, of course, but it's also been a joy for me that Bart's former boss Wayne has become a close friend. He and his wife Aiwei, their young son Theo, who is Franklin's age, and little baby Mia just shared New Year's with our family at our home. I've also kept in close contact with Brian, who had been Wayne's boss at Micron and a good friend of our family. A couple of months ago John and I attended the baptism of Brian and his wife Kathryn's baby girl. They live in Singapore now, but when they return we intend to get together as often as possible with Brian and his family, along with Wayne and his family. These relationships that bridge past and present mean so much to me.

Like my good friends Kelly and Martha, my sister Jody, and others who have known me well, Wayne has told me how far I have come in my grief recovery. People say they're proud of me. And after reading through all my journals and retracing my healing steps for this book, I also feel proud of who I've become. I finally feel confident much of the time and more like a normal person than ever. I am in love with Franklin, who is such a beautiful, smart boy. And John is an amazing dad! The love John and I share may sometimes feel different from what I am used to, but it's real, and I pray to God every day that we may continue to grow even closer.

In the days and weeks leading up to the tenth anniversary of the accident, waves of sadness swept over me. I spent many an hour when John and Franklin were out listening to my Italy video just allowing myself to cry, then applying makeup to cover my swollen eyes. But I spent several days around the time of the anniversary in San Diego with John and Franklin, and it was a surprisingly good trip. I cried a bit but also came back with many happy memories.

Before we left for San Diego, I had looked up Saturday markets there because I'd always enjoyed seeing the local talent and interests at the one we have in Boise and others I've visited in cities around the world. On the Internet, the top-rated Saturday event in San Diego that popped up was Mercato: Little Italy's Farmers' Market. It had to have been fate! I didn't push it, but John seemed as excited as I was. He understood that in Little Italy I would naturally feel closer to Bart, Benjamin, and Samuel.

While there we picked out some beautiful fresh flowers for our room, shared a glass of blood orange juice, and bought some homemade olive oil. John carried Franklin on his shoulders, as Bart would Samuel, while we surveyed the fresh produce and the beautiful art and jewels. Franklin loved the accordion player and the other musicians enlivening the market. It all made me feel extremely close as one whole family—past and present.

When we stopped for lunch at Café Zucchero's, I spent several minutes just staring at the menu, appreciating how much it reminded me of our many meals in Italy. After sorting through the homemade pastas, I admired the beautiful desserts before choosing two scoops of gelato: coconut and lemon, flavors I knew my "boys" would have liked.

The next day we took Franklin swimming and then off to view a navy ship. We had brought our sitter Tabitha along for the trip, so that night John and I were able to share a private dinner at a beautiful Italian restaurant in the Gaslamp District. Afterward, while listening to music in Jim Croce's piano bar, I cried as we began to talk about the accident and how unfair it was that Bart and the boys were gone. Then John spoke about his feelings of how normal it is to have them all a part of our family. We toasted them with a glass of delicious armorone, a red wine. Slowly, my spirits rose. As we started talking about the upcoming year, I realized how excited I really was about our future. At one point we brought up the idea of each us having two cursive Js tattooed around our ring finger, as a symbol of infinity. Neither of us has ever had a tattoo, but if the five-star tattoo shop we found on the Internet had been open we would have done it...maybe we still will.

On our way back to Boise, I felt even more strongly that the passing of the tenth anniversary of the accident had been one more important step in grief recovery and in saying good-bye and moving forward. It's almost as if I am really just starting my future. It's not that Bart and the boys will not be a part of me daily; I will always hear their voices and feel their presence. But I now feel present. I feel whole. For the first time in ten years, I really want to be in my current life. I am excited about sharing my experiences as a way to help others, though I can't yet completely shake the nervousness that comes with this excitement. I am especially elated to be here for John and Franklin and I can't wait to see what life has to offer us!

I know logically that my current life could end in a tragic way as it did before, but I understand now that I have a choice whether to focus on the pain and sorrow, which will never go away, or live a healthy, content, and largely happy life. I know that only the person suffering can make this decision, and it can only be done when the fog lifts. My initial outlook was something like this: "I cannot bring them back, so there is nothing I can do to fix my life." Now, after much effort and time, my perspective looks more like this: "Life sometimes sucks, which I can either accept and use to gain strength or choose to let it bury me."

When I'm feeling especially confident about the future, I imagine new ventures I may yet experience. I'm eager to continue speaking appearances, visiting with all kinds of groups and organizations. I've even envisioned establishing a foundation I would call KRAFT, for Keeping Responsible Adolescents Focused Today. I would love the opportunity to help young people, whether near my home, where I grew up, or in places like the orphanage at Sacro Coure in Italy.

After all those agonizing months when I wanted my life on earth to end as soon as possible so I could join Bart and the boys in heaven, I've come to realize that I'm going to be around quite a while yet and must keep figuring out how to follow my new life purpose. That means continuing to listen to that Bart-ism: "Make yourself happy and others around you will be happy." These days I have found more ways to make myself happy. I'm also a lot more independent and fun, less concerned with the tomorrows in life, and better able to live for the moment.

Epilogue
The Mirror Made Clear

IT'S BEEN A TYPICAL DAY *in my routine with Franklin: 6:30 am—Woke up and got ready; 7:00—woke Franklin, got him ready, fed him, fixed his late morning snack; 7:30—piled into the car and headed for McCall, fifty minutes away, making sure Franklin's fire dog Rescue and his polka-dot blanket were with him; 8:00—dropped Frankin off at Mountain Life Preschool; 9:00—went to the Hub for one more cup of coffee; 10:00—worked out with Kerry, our trainer, at the local gym; 12:00 noon—picked up Franklin from school; 1:00—arrived home and fixed a quick lunch; 2:00—played with Franklin outside; 4:00—started thinking about dinner while Franklin and Daddy had some "guy time"; 5:30—had dinner; 6:00—gave Franklin a bath and told him stories; 7:00—put Franklin to bed, then cleaned up.*

As I pick up Franklin's clothes off the bathroom floor, I glance into the mirror. I clearly see myself as I am today. For so long I have felt disconnected from the woman in the mirrored image I had observed, usually with great pain, as if observing another person. But now I see myself as whole, my family, past and present, united. I see hope. I see a mischievous little boy sleeping. I see a fun-loving husband who helps me appreciate each day and embraces my memories of Mom, Sarah, Benjamin, Samuel, and even Bart, viewing them as part of his family. I see faith and confidence that come from within. I see a woman who continues to be challenged but whose feet are facing in the right direction and who is now taking more steps forward than backward. I see a woman who will always face new challenges, yet who, with the help of others and God, has found tools to keep her head above the unending wave of grief. ⬳

To learn more about the author, visit her Web site at
www.findingjill.com.

To inquire about her availability as a speaker, please send correspondence to:

Jill Kraft Thompson
227 Morgan Drive
McCall, ID 83638

Made in the USA
Charleston, SC
14 November 2016